PEOPLE AND PLACES
IN THE STORY OF
THE SCOTTISH CHURCH

PEOPLE AND PLACES
IN THE STORY OF
THE SCOTTISH CHURCH

EDWIN SPROTT TOWILL

Illustrated by Colin Gibson

THE SAINT ANDREW PRESS
EDINBURGH

To
Cousin
JOHN CHAPPELL SPROTT
Bishop of Brechin
1959–1975

I have only made a nosegay of culled flowers and have brought nothing of my own but the string which ties them.

Montaigne

Homo sum; humani nil a me alienum puto.   Terence

Considering the difficulty there is for those who wish to enter upon the narratives of history because of the mass of material, we have aimed to please those who wish to read, to make it easy for those who are inclined to memorize, and to profit all readers. For us who have undertaken the toil of abbreviating, it is no light matter, but calls for sweat and loss of sleep. It is the duty of the original historian to discuss matters from every side and to take trouble with details, but the one who recasts the narrative should be allowed to strive for brevity of expression. At this point therefore let us begin our narrative, for it is foolish to lengthen the preface while cutting short the history itself.

2 Maccabees 2

First published in 1976 by
THE SAINT ANDREW PRESS
121 George Street, Edinburgh

© Edwin Sprott Towill 1976

ISBN 0 7152 0252 9 (Limp)
ISBN 0 7152 0322 3 (Cased)

Printed in Great Britain by
Robert MacLehose and Company Limited
Printers to the University of Glasgow

CONTENTS

PREFACE

This book is not meant to be either a biographical dictionary or a gazetteer of Scottish places. It is much more subjective: most of the people in the notes are those who have attracted or repelled me, but all of whom have fascinated me. The reader will quickly discover that they are not all saints. Some were great sinners and a few were probably quite mad. But each played some small part in the story of the Scottish Church — that is, if you accept 'Church' in the broadest sense, as I have done. Not only have I included all the respectable denominations but also a number of people who manufactured their own variety or deviation of Christianity. I pray that no reader will imagine that the inclusion of a note on anyone indicates that I homologate their theology or sing Te Deums of thanks for their contribution to the Church Militant. I have even dared to include two or three pre-Christian persons and several who laboured mainly outwith Scotland.

It is the same with places: the length of the note bears no relation to the importance of the place. Some very important places are merely referred to, or not mentioned at all. In such cases the reader will find plenty of good guide books available. My selection has been first from places which had some special point of interest, or those which I had come to know personally in the course of a life which has taken me into most corners of Scotland. I have gone beyond the borders of Scotland when this seemed necessary, as in the case of the Northumbrian Church and the Irish Church, both of which were closely linked with our history. I could, of course, have continued with more people and more places almost indefinitely, but my publisher had, quite rightly, to call a halt.

For whom do I look as readers? First, I am sure that there are very many people all over Scotland who want in a handy form some information about those who built the churches in their town or district, who separated to form a new denomination, or who for a brief while attracted the crowds and made the parish famous. Such information has not been come by easily. The stories of the front-line figures have been told over and over again, but the less important people are, I find, often more interesting and are in some danger today of being forgotten except by a few scholars.

Secondly, I hope that this book will be a help to many visitors who desire something deeper than the glossy, highly-coloured booklets displayed so prominently in our multiple bookshops. Churches and Christian thought in Scotland have been 'different' in many ways, historically and today — and visitors want to know why. Here they should find a little about the highways and quite a lot about the byways of Scottish life as it related to the things of the spirit.

The third class of reader I have in mind is of growing importance. 'Environmental Studies' has now rightly taken its place in senior schools and colleges of education. I myself have been relating the story of the Church to the story of the environment in school and in college for almost twenty years and it is really from this experience that the book has grown. Increasingly I found frustration in the shortage of handy material for projects for my pupils and, later, my students. I did not gather all the materials myself but worked on the principle of sending them out to explore and discover as part of their project. My pupils crossed rivers, climbed mountains, and cycled scores of miles until (literally) the bicycle disintegrated under one of them in the search for many of the facts gathered here. I suppose that this book ought really to have been dedicated, not to my reverend kinsman, but to the fifth-form girl (where is she now?) who ventured across into Cumberland to find if there actually was a Ninian's Well near St Martin's Church at Old Brampton. She sent a letter back to school: 'There is. I fell down the slope and landed in it!' I hope, then, that these notes may be of use to a new generation in school and college.

I realise that there must be some errors and for these, please blame no one but myself. I am greatly indebted to my friend and former student, Mr Huisdean A. M. Duff, M.A., for reading the manuscript and, from his compendious knowledge of the Scottish Church, making invaluable corrections and suggestions. Among many clergy and others who have loaned material or provided facilities I would mention only Fr Hanlon of St Theresa's Roman Catholic Church, Dundee, and the Rev John Clifford of Glasgow Unitarian Church. I am glad that the publishers have chosen my old friend Colin Gibson of Monifieth to prepare the cover design and the illustrations, which so artistically supplement my text. At The Saint Andrew Press I would thank Mr T. B. Honeyman for first seeing some value in the manuscript and Mr Maurice Berrill and Mr John Geekie for sympathetically steering it through the processes of publication.

* * * * *

In the text, † signifies that the person or place is the subject of a separate entry, to which reference should be made for further information.

AM = Ancient Monument under the Department of the Environment.
NTS = Property in the care of the National Trust for Scotland.
G.R. = National Grid Reference, given for a place off the beaten track.
[. . .] = An earlier or alternative form of the name.

After 'places' in the text, except for burghs which are big enough to be generally known, the county has been given (in parentheses); although the old county names do not now have any official significance, for long we shall use them for locations. On the other hand, in the *Geographical Index of Places* on pp. xiii–xvii, we have arranged the entries according to the new Regions since students, who may be most likely to make use of this index, will find that their projects are related to the new boundaries system.

In the *Chronological Index of People* on pp. ix–xii, persons whose work seems important in two centuries have their names shown twice.

EDWIN SPROTT TOWILL

BIBLIOGRAPHY AND SOURCES

Limitations of space have made it impossible for me to give references to my authorities, much as I had desired to do this. In a few cases I have interrupted the text to refer to sources but to do so more frequently was not practicable. For almost all persons of the seventeenth century and later there exist standard biographies which are available in major reference libraries. The *Dictionary of National Biography*, the *Fasti Ecclesiae Scoticanae* (and the corresponding clergy lists for the other denominations), and the *First* and the *Second Statistical Accounts* are all invaluable. The *Oxford Dictionary of the Christian Church* (second edition, Cross and Livingstone) is helpful where it provides an entry.

Sources for the 'Celtic' period are most difficult for the general reader since many are in Middle Irish or Mediaeval Latin and most of the general histories or textbooks simply re-hash the traditional pictures of the saints built up from mediaeval *Lives*. Furthermore, scholarship today moves so quickly that theses and theories accepted a few years ago may now be outdated. Anything by Charles Thomas, Kenneth Jackson, Isobel Henderson or Nora Chadwick — and the list might well be extended to Mayr-Harting, E. G. Bowen and some others — may be accepted almost without question, while anything by W. D. Simpson or G. F. Knight, although valuable, should be regarded with reservation. Skene is outdated; A. B. Scott doubtful in almost all his statements.

The *Proceedings of the Society of Antiquaries of Scotland* are excellent for detailed study of places, as are also the *Transactions of the Dumfries and Galloway Natural History and Antiquarian Society*, the *Books of the Old Edinburgh Club*, and other local historical society publications. The various guidebooks to abbeys and ancient monuments published by Her Majesty's Stationery Office should not be despised because they are in paperback; they are scholarly yet handy.

The number of modern topographical books for Scotland is not nearly as great nor are they as detailed in content as those for England, but the volumes in the *Highways and Byways* series, although they lead one through scenery now much altered, are still helpful. A later series is *The Queen's Scotland* and new series are now beginning to appear though many are lacking in precise detail. We shall never again see the full parish histories often written by ministers of the last century; consult them whenever you can.

The Scots Magazine has for long been a fund of information on local history, aided to a lesser extent by *Scottish Field* and *Scotland's Magazine*. England now has several publishing firms issuing locally really serious material, biographical and topographical; until very recently we had nothing to offer visitors to Scotland but glossy, highly-coloured booklets, with what little text there was restricting itself to incidents in the lives of 'Prince Charlie' or Mary, Queen of Scots. At last there are welcome signs of a breakthrough, largely in the north of Scotland, with such small but serious efforts as *Caithness Notebooks*, *Protheroe Books*, the publications of the Inverness Field Club and the Fortrose Press, or the more official *Scottish Archaeological Forum*. For Roman Catholic history there is the *Innes Review* and Peter Anson's *Underground Catholicism in Scotland, 1622–1878*. There are also the *Proceedings of the Scottish Ecclesiological Society* and similar journals. J. H. S. Burleigh's *Church History of Scotland* is useful but skims over movements not linked to the main stream of national Presbyterianism. Reference may be made to Harry Escott's *A History of Scottish Congregationalism*, to George Yuille's *History of the Baptists in*

Scotland or the work by Derek B. Murray on that denomination, and to the old regulars, *Annals of the Original Secession*, *Annals of the Disruption*, etc., for branches of Presbyterianism. For the Episcopal Church, in addition to the separate biographies of the various bishops, Marion Lochhead's *Episcopal Scotland in the Nineteenth Century* is packed with fact told as happily as if it were fiction.

CHRONOLOGICAL INDEX OF PEOPLE

A. Pre-Christian, Early Christian (Celtic) to Saxon.

ADAMNAN
AIDAN of Lindisfarne
AIDAN macGABRAIN
ALEXANDER I
ARTHUR

BLANE
BOISIL
BONIFACE
BRIDE or BRIGIT
BRUIDE macDERILE

CATAN
CEOLFRID
COLMAN of Dromore
COLMAN of Lindisfarne
COLUMBA [Colum-cille]
COMGALL
CONCHUBAR
CONSTANTINE (Saint)
CORMAC
CURITAN
CUTHBERT

DAVID [Dewi]
DEIRDRE
DONEVALDUS
DROSTAN

EATA
ERTHA

FERADACH

GUINEVERE [Vanora]

KENNETH [Cainnech]
KENTIGERN [Cynderyn; Mungo]

LOTH

MACCUIL [Maughold]
MIRREN
MOCHAOI
MODWENNA
MORKEN

NECHTAN macDERILE
NINIAN [Nyniau]

OSWALD
OSWY

PALLADIUS
PATRICK
PAULINUS
PECHTHELM
PENDA

REDERICH
REGULUS [Rule]

SEGINE
SERF [Servanus]

THENEW
TRIDUANA
TRISTRAM

B. Mediaeval (to c. 1520; omitting persons classed as 'Reformation')

BALIOL, John
BOECE, Hector
deBOTHWELL, Richard

COMYN, Walter, Earl of Menteith
CRAWFORD, Sir John

DEVORGILLA
DUNCAN, Earl of Carrick
DUNS SCOTUS, John

ELPHINSTONE, William

GILES [Egidius]

HENRYSON, Josina

JOCELYN of Furness

deKELDELETI•, Robert

LAUDER, Thomas

MACDOUGALL, Duncan, of Lorn
MALACHY [Maelmadoc]
MARGARET

REID, Robert
ROSE, Hugh, of Kilravock

SETON, Janet, Lady

WYNTOUN, Andrew of

C. Reformation and Seventeenth Century (Presbytery v Episcopacy)

D. Eighteenth Century

E. Nineteenth Century and after

GEOGRAPHICAL INDEX OF PLACES

Arranged according to the new Regions. For convenience Strathclyde and Lotkians have been subdivided, but not into the official Districts.

HIGHLAND
Including Orkney, Shetland and the Western Isles

AVOCH [Kilcurdy]

BALLACHULISH
BEAULY PRIORY

CROMARTY
CULLODEN

DUN DEARDUIL

FEARN ABBEY

GEDDES
GLENFINNAN
GLEN URQUHART

INVERNESS

KEISS
KILRAVOCK

LOCH INSCH
LOCH MORAR
LOCH NESS

PAPA WESTRAY
PORTMAHOMACK

RAASAY, Isle of
ROSEMARKIE

ST BRIDE'S EPISCOPAL CHURCH, LOCHABER
ST JOHN'S EPISCOPAL CHURCH, BALLACHULISH
ST MARY'S EPISCOPAL CHURCH, GLENCOE
SHIELDAIG
STORNOWAY (Nicolson Institute)

THURSO

GRAMPIAN

ABERDEEN
ABOYNE
AQUHORTIES

BANFF
BLAIRS COLLEGE
BRANDSBUTT PICTISH STONE
BURGHEAD

CABRACH
CHAPEL of GARIOCH
CHAPEL of the CRAIGS

DEER
DUNNOTTAR

FETTERCAIRN
FORDOUN
FRASERBURGH
FYVIE

GORDONSTOUN

HUNTLY

INVERURIE

KINELLAR
KING'S COLLEGE, ABERDEEN
KINMUCK
KINTORE CHURCHYARD

LINSHART
LOGIE ELPHINSTONE
LUTHERMUIR

MAIDEN STONE

PETERCULTER
PLUSCARDEN PRIORY

RATHVEN

ST GILES' CHURCH, ELGIN
ST PETER'S ROMAN CATHOLIC CHURCH, ABERDEEN
SAUCHIEBURN
SCALAN

URY

TAYSIDE

FIFE

LOTHIANS

(i) Edinburgh City

(ii) Landward

BORDERS

DUMFRIES AND GALLOWAY

FURTH OF SCOTLAND

(i) England and Wales

(ii) Ireland

PEOPLE AND PLACES
IN THE STORY OF
THE SCOTTISH CHURCH

A—Z

ABDIE KIRK (Fife). Hidden in the gusset between A913 and A983 is the new kirk of Abdie, itself now a century and a half old. Hidden again behind it the visitor will find the old kirk, a neatly preserved, ivy-clad ruin of considerable interest and charm. The name suggests the dependency of an abbey and as the kirk is older than the nearby Tironian monastery of Lindores it doubtless refers to the Celtic foundation of Abernethy†. It was rededicated in 1242 by Bishop de Bernham and the fabric has been remodelled several times, but never cruelly. The Pictish slab which formerly stood at the side of the main road, in such a position that antiquarians could only view it at peril of their lives, is now preserved in the gatehouse. At some period the Lindores monks superimposed the hours on the original symbol to use it as a sun-dial, and in the nineteenth century it was further disfigured by a bench-mark. There are monuments to Balfours of Denholm (Sir James was comptroller to Charles I and his son was Lyon King and a noted antiquarian) and to Admiral Maitland who captained the *Bellerophon* when she took on board the defeated Napoleon. The old kirk is more worthy of a visit than the nearby Lindores Abbey of which only fragments remain — and these are often guarded by a bull.

ABERDEEN. *See* Elphinstone, William; Forbes, Patrick; Skinner, John; Rutherford, Samuel.

ABERLADY [Aberlessic]. *See* Thenew.

ABERLEMNO (Angus). Four Pictish crosses, the finest of which is off B9134 within the kirkyard. Such monuments are divided into three classes: 1, those bearing only pagan symbols, usually roughly incised; 2, with such symbols but having in addition a cross or other Christian symbols, often carefully shaped and carved in relief; 3, with only Christian or Bible symbols. The stone in Aberlemno kirkyard is the finest of all Class 2 stones; on one side a great wheeled cross and intricate Celtic interlacing and animals; on the reverse, in addition to the typical Pictish symbols, a great battle scene with most lifelike figures. Dr W. Douglas Simpson writes 'It is hard to resist the conclusion that a real battle, a definite historical event is here commemorated and that beneath this monument sleeps a chieftain of high rank slain in conflict nearby; Boece, after detailing the battle of Restenneth tells that the fallen king Feradach was buried at Forfar . . . It is just conceivable that if not Feradach, at least one of his chiefs lies here . . .' At the roadside are three more slabs: one badly weathered, a second (Class 1) with incised symbols and a great Class 2 with a cross nearly 10 feet high, supported by little angels in postures of devotion and pagan symbols on the obverse side. The earliest of these stones was here a century before Saint Curitan† brought Christianity to Restenneth†.

ABERNETHY (Perthshire). Nearby, on the banks of the Tay, the Romans built their fort at Carpow, which Butler, the historian of Abernethy, believes was Ptolemy's Orrea. Later it became the capital of the Southern Pictish tribe(s) with perhaps a fort on The Law. According to a rather suspect tradition Ninian established a muinntir or community here and Columba refounded it, so bringing both the leading saints into the picture. The dedication, however, is to Bridget; the Pictish Chronicle refers to a gift of land by Nachtan 'unto God and St. Briget until judgement day'. Local place names include St Bride's Seat, a Ninewells (Ninian?) and a Brendi Well which refers to St Brendan. History here is as suspect as in many other

The Round Tower, Abernethy

Scottish places for it was later thoroughly 'gone over' by the Roman monks to make it acceptable. There are, however, tangible memorials of the Pictish period in typical symbol stones at Abdie† and in the churchyard wall at Abernethy, and some slightly later stones and crosses (Mugdrum estate). Also, of course, there is the great round tower, one of only two which remain in Scotland. That at Brechin may date from the eighth century but the Abernethy tower is probably three centuries later. Ireland has a great many such towers but their purpose is still a subject for argument by scholars; it is accepted that they were for defence against the Norsemen and Danes but were also used as bell-towers. Unfortunately the Abernethy tower, having lost its cap, is more ridiculous in appearance than impressive. In the life of St Wilfred there is mention of a battle at Abernethy in 672 between Angles and Picts about 40 years before Nechtansmere when the Anglians were finally driven back. About this time the Roman customs were adopted and the capital may have been removed to Scone. It has been suggested that the foundation continued but was reorganised on Roman lines. There is an obscure local legend of nine daughters of St Donevald who were given a place to retire at Abernethy after labouring in Glen Ogilvy. Some interesting but forgotten piece of folk-lore must lie behind the story. For the history of Abernethy in the time of Moncrieff† the seceder, see the note on his life, and that on Brown, John.

ABOYNE. *See* Adamnan.

ADAMNAN [Adomnan; Eunan; Thewnan; Arnold; Skeulan etc.]. *c.* 624–704. Ninth Ab of Iona. Born in Donegal just 27 years after the death of the great founder, of whose clan, the Ui Neills, he was also a member. His name, 'Wee Adam', is found in a variety of forms confusing to us but legitimate in Gaelic. He joined the Iona community while his kinsman, Segine, was leader. In 679 at the age of 55 he succeeded to the responsibility of Ab. He was a close friend of (and probably anamcaraidh or soul-friend to) the Northumbrian prince Ealdfrith who had been educated in Ireland and Iona as Flann Fina macOssa, and so he visited Northumbria and came under the influence of the Romanizing clerics whose party, opposed to the Celtic practices, was in the ascendancy. A second visit in 688 saw his adoption of the Roman tonsure and calendar, and under his influence the Columban monasteries in Ireland conformed. The parent community, however, refused to follow him and thereafter he avoided controversy by dwelling mostly in Ireland, returning to Iona only shortly before his death. Adamnan was the most scholarly of the Columban Abs — his biography of Columba in three parts (prophecies or revelations, miracles and visions) ranks among the world's great books. In judging such works we must remember that they are not biographies in the modern sense, but 'hagiography', glorifications of the saint with stress on the miraculous. In another work, *De Locis Sanctis* Adamnan provided for pilgrims a guide to the Holy Land without having been there himself, working up the stories of a visitor who had returned in the manner of a modern literary 'ghost'. He is also noted in Irish history as the leading figure at the Synod of Birr in 697, which by the 'Cain Adomnain' elevated the position of women and gave them special privileges. In Scotland there are many wells, hills, churches etc. which bear his name in one of its several forms: St Arnold's Seat at Tannadice which in the sixteenth century was St Eunendi's Seat; St Theunan's Church at Aboyne; Tom Eunan near Loch Insch at Kingussie; Ardeonaig by Loch Tay and others. Some may represent places visited personally by the saint but, as with all the early Celtic missionaries, many such links may indicate nothing more than the presence of an altar in mediaeval times. *See also* Curitan.

ADAMS, William. *See* Gillespie, Thomas.

AGNEW, Sir Andrew, Bart, of Lochnaw. 1793–1849. The Agnews came to the Rhinns as Norman conquerors and became Hereditary Sheriffs of Galloway. In Covenanting times the then Sir Andrew was fined for failing to 'take The Test' and his sheriffdom given to Graham of Claverhouse. The 7th baronet was born posthumously and brought up with his mother's family, the de Courcy's of Kinsale, in Ireland. He inherited at 16, settled down

Sir Andrew Agnew

to improve the Lochnaw estate which had fallen into poor condition and represented Wigtownshire in Parliament, 1830–7. He married Madeline, daughter of Sir David Carnegie of Southesk, a lady of religious temperament who greatly influenced her husband. Sir Andrew, at this distance of time, would make an excellent subject for a sociological and psychological inquiry into the causes which turned an affable country gentleman into a fanatic for Sabbath Observance. Macaulay said 'We know no spectacle so ridiculous as the British public in one of its periodical fits of morality' and Sir Andrew was caught up in one such period and illustrates the wave of puritanism which was well begun before Victoria and Albert joined in, and for which they got the blame. The change in public attitude toward the new puritanism is seen in the reception which Sir Andrew's parliamentary bills received in the House; at first there was lighthearted derision — such as the lampoon delivered against him by O'Connell —

'. . . One
Who hanged his wicked cat on Monday,
Because she killed a mouse on Sunday.'

— or forthright opposition; but within a few years the temper of the majority was with him and in his time, or shortly afterwards, all the Sabbatarian laws were passed which only today are being questioned. Sunday trading and pleasure excursions of all kinds were, of course, forbidden, mail coaches halted and 'strict orders were given at the royal palace that all provisions for Sunday should be got in on the preceding Saturday'. At Lochnaw, long after the 7th baronet's day it was still the custom to have cold food and for all in the castle except the elderly ladies to walk the two miles to church. After Sir Andrew was defeated and retired from Parliament he continued to act as President of a host of Lord's Day Societies and to chair meetings in furtherance of his favourite cause. At the age of 56 he caught scarlet fever and died at his Edinburgh home in Rutland Square. He is buried in Grange Cemetery beside one of his great heroes and friends, Dr Chalmers. The Ulster ferries, as they sail up Loch Ryan from Stranraer, pass, on the Rhinns side, the tall tower erected by his tenants to his memory. When he first came to Lochnaw he made many additions to the old castle and did so in such a way that it could be demolished later without affecting the newer parts. Such are the vagaries of time that today his rebuilding and additions have been pulled down while the original keep stands much as he found it.

AIDAN. d. 651. Monk of Iona in the abbacy of Segine, fourth in succession from Columba. When Oswald, who had been exiled in Iona, became king of Northumbria after his victory at Heavenfield, near Hexham, he desired to re-establish Christianity in his dominions and turned not to Canterbury, whence Paulinus had led the first mission to Northumbria in Edwin's reign, but to the Celtic 'familia' of which Iona was the leading monastery. Bede relates that the first missioner had returned dispirited when a young monk, Aidan, offered himself for the task. King and saint worked closely together, at first from the capital fortress Bebbanburgh or Bamburgh, and then from the island Celtic-type monastery Lindisfarne, formerly called Innis Medcant. Christianity was firmly established in Northumbria with this 'eastern Iona' as its centre; it was to create for Christian art the most beautiful of all Celtic manuscripts, and from it the great archepiscopal diocese of York was later to develop. The partnership of Oswald and Aidan was tragically brief. In 642 the king

Aidan — the statue by Kathleen Parbury on Holy Island

was killed by Penda of Mercia at Oswestry on the Welsh border. Oswy, his brother and successor in Bernicia (for Northumbria had been divided) was equally helpful to Aidan but it was a time of war and unrest. Looking from the island monastery over to the fortress the saint saw the flames of the burning capital. In 651, back in Bamburgh, Aidan, worn out and tired, died quietly, leaning against a beam of the church he had founded. The spot is still held in respect in Bamburgh church today and beside it a window depicts the first meeting of Oswald and Aidan.

AIDAN macGABRAIN. *See* Arthur.

AIKMAN, John. d. 1834. Friend and associate of James Haldane†. Assisted in the services at the Edinburgh Circus and (later) the Tabernacle, and then at his own expense built the North College Street Chapel, later called Argyll Square Chapel and eventually transferred to George IV Bridge as Augustine Congregational Church. He ministered in this 'dark, dingy, comfortless place' without stipend (he had been a wealthy West-Indian merchant) until his death. He would not follow the Haldanes when they adopted the principle of 'believers' baptism' and so is regarded as one of the founders of Scottish congregationalism; he was the first president of the Union in 1812. He was fluent in languages, preaching in German and founding a congregational church at Hamburg, and at home in Edinburgh he ministered to the Napoleonic prisoners in the Castle.

AILEACH AN NAOIMH [Hinba?] (Garvelloch Isles, off Oban). Small, rocky isle, difficult of access except in good weather. Very early stone remains, perhaps as early as Columba's time, have been protected by their inaccessibility but have suffered through weathering. In 1930 the Glasgow Archaeological Society visited the island and identified a chapel, a beehive cell, an oast house and perhaps a small monastery in addition to graves. Other, later buildings, probably connected with sheep farming, made positive identification difficult. The hill dominating the island is Dun Bhreanain, or Brendan's Hill, and there is no doubt that this is the Aillach of that saint's life. More doubt exists about its connection with Columba. In Adamnan's *Life* there are seven references to a place called Hinba with which Aileach an Naoimh has usually been identified, but on geographical grounds some scholars would place Hinba out among the western isles, or at Colonsay and Oronsay†. Note that the correct version of the island in Gaelic is 'aileach' = rock, not 'eilean' = island, and 'an', not 'na', identifies it with one saint, i.e. The Rock of the Saint. If it be Hinba then it was here, at 'The Mass of the Saints' that Brendan saw a brilliant light over the head of Columba, who was celebrating in the presence of Comgall, Cormac, Cainnech† and himself. The island appears to have been a place of penance for monks from Iona under discipline and it would form a useful outpost, linking the parent muinntir or community with the mainland. One grave, apart by itself, is reputed (but without evidence) to be that of Eithne, mother of Columba.

AIRTHREY (Stirlingshire). *See* Logie Airth; Serf.

ALEXANDER I. *See* Restenneth.

ALL SAINTS CHURCH, TOLLCROSS, EDINBURGH. *See* Chinnery-Haldane.

ALVA. *See* Serf.

ANGUS, John. 1515–96. Benedictine monk, Precentor and Almoner of Dunfermline Abbey during the Reformation period. He is often credited with the metrical psalm tune 'Dunfermline'; while there is no proof of his authorship it was composed within his period and its title suggests he might well have been its composer. He played a large part in the preparation of the new psalter but his main work was the composition of suitably singable tunes for the canticles and the metrical version of the psalms. Ten of these are extant and it is a pity that they are not sung today — they include 'The Simboll or Creide of Athanasius', 'The Sang of the Blessit Virgin' and 'The Song of the Thre Childring'. It has been suggested that Angus anticipated the Reformation in music by providing metrical pieces which the people could sing in the vernacular. This would have been dangerous at a time when the authorities were seeking out heretics and it is unlikely that Abbot Durie† would have permitted such innovations. More likely he continued in the abbey church under its first Protestant minister, David Ferguson, and composed for the new type of services. We know that he was appointed vicar of Inverkeithing (1562) and parson at Crieff (1595) but these were probably titular offices without duties — a common device to provide such as he with a small pension. It is also said that he had a living or a pension in connection with the Chapel Royal at Stirling; this may have been because of his musical talents but no definite facts are known about it. One of his fellow compilers of the metrical psalter describes John Angus as 'gude and meike' and he may be considered representative of a large number of sincere servants of the 'auld faith' who, without any sense of hypocrisy, could embrace the Reformed interpretation of Christian worship and doctrine.

ANNAN. *See* Irving, Edward.

ANWOTH (Stewartry of Kirkcudbright). *See* Rutherford, Samuel.

AQUHORTIES. *See* Scalan.

ARBIRLOT (Angus). *See* Guthrie, Thomas; Kirk, John.

ARBROATH. *See* Wesley, John; Lee, Robert.

ARDCHATTAN PRIORY (Argyll; AM). Founded in 1230 by Duncan Macdougall of Lorn. By an irony of history, it is said to have been the scene in 1308 of a Council at which Robert Bruce won the support of the Gaelic chieftains — crucial to his cause — with the exception of the Macdougalls, his inveterate enemies. Unlike Beauly† and Pluscarden†, the other two Valliscaulian priories, which later became respectively Cistercian and Benedictine, Ardchattan always remained Valliscaulian. The last Prior was Alexander Campbell and at the Reformation the Priory fell under the domination of his family. The buildings were severely damaged in the seventeenth century in the Montrose and the Cromwellian troubles. The choir survives though its walls stand nowhere higher than six feet. Some late mediaeval grave slabs are preserved and in a late burial vault stands a cross-slab which may be as old as the Priory itself.

ARDEONAIG (Loch Tay). *See* Adamnan.

ARDWALL ISLE (Galloway; G.R. NX 573495). In 1964–5 Charles Thomas made a thorough excavation of this small island, one of the four Isles of Fleet, separated from the Galloway mainland by a narrow strip of shallow sea. Forty years earlier workmen had unearthed a cross-slab of about eleventh century date, but the new excavations were to reveal Celtic church remains many centuries earlier. The island, in size only about ½ x ¼ mile, is now uninhabited but showed what to the trained eye appeared to be an early British type Christian cemetery and a little chapel, called by the Irish and Alban Celts a 'cill', by the Manx 'keill', by the Welsh 'llan' and by the Cornish 'lan'. It was resolved to dig below the early stone remains to see if the post-holes of any primitive wooden buildings might be found. The foundations of the first buildings to be uncovered, and therefore the latest by date, showed them to be a smugglers' tavern of about late eighteenth century. Below this were the foundations of a sturdy keep about 1300 in

date. Below this again there were no less than three distinct Celtic Christian settlements. The lowest, the last to be revealed, was a small cemetery of disintegrated skeletons, obviously clustered round a semi-subterranean shrine which might have held a wooden casket with a saint's or founder's bones. This would indicate the reinterment of the revered figure — a common practice — and so, not necessarily in this island, there must have been an even earlier Christian phase. Above this primitive stratum lay a more organized cemetery, and the post-holes of a 'cill' with an accompanying stone shrine. With the exception of one child the bones were all adult male, including one old man with arthritis. Obviously these were remains of Celtic monks. The posts of the wooden chapel had been driven down through the earlier cemetery. Above all this came the final Celtic phase — a small but well built chapel of local stone. The remains of the altar were skilfully recovered and appeared to hold within the cavity the remains of a person, who must have been held in high honour to have this position. Was he the original founder? Had these remains occupied in turn the two earlier shrines? One other large stone in this top Celtic phase was important — a great cross slab with the name CUDGAR. Important as he must have been he could not have been the founder for not only is the name Anglian, not British or Gaelic, but the cross and the lettering could not date earlier than the uppermost of the three phases. It is scarcely necessary to emphasize the importance of the Ardwall discoveries. The evidence is more convincing than anything that can be postulated about Whithorn. It would, however, be unwise to speculate at this stage just how it fits into the picture of what we have called elsewhere 'the Solway Mission' of the early British Church.

ARTHUR. fl. c. AD 500. The justification for giving King Arthur a place here among notable religious figures, lies in (*a*) the tradition that he represented the Roman-British Christian hero opposing the pagan Saxons, and (*b*) the much later fully-developed Arthurian legend, widespread throughout Europe, that with his knights he founded a chivalric society based on

Christian faith and values. In the territory which is now Scotland, there are many place names commemorating the hero: the famous Arthur's Seat in the capital with another in Angus; in the latter county also is Arthur's Fold and his Stone. He is said to have sheltered in Arthur's Cave in the Eildon Hills. Lanark has his Fountain, Stirling his Oven and a Round Table, while Camelon claims to be Camelot. Ben Arthur is in Dunbartonshire and Arthurhouse in Kincardineshire. Peebles has a Merlin's Cave, while our note on Meiglet gives the tradition of Guinevere and Mordred. Modern scholarship, however, has generally insisted that his habitat (if there ever was an Arthur at all) lay in the West Country of England: perhaps as far north as Wales or as far west as Cornwall, but centred on Somerset. Glastonbury connections which used to be dismissed have been stressed by Alcock, Ashe and others and the recent large-scale excavations at South Cadbury have produced suggestions that it was Camelot in spite of the fact that nothing was unearthed, either there or at corresponding digs at Mere and at Glastonbury Tor to connect any of these places with Arthur. The case for a northern Arthur has recently been restated by Richard Barber (*The Figure of Arthur*, London 1972). Basing his theory on a mention in the *Gododdin* (the Welsh epic by Aneirin) and on Adamnan's *Life of Columba*, with support from the *Annals* of Tigernach — all three tip-top authorities — he takes Arthur to be one of the three sons of Aidan macGabrain of Dalriada — 'Artuir, Echoid Find and Domingart'. This Scotic prince whom Barber calls 'Arthur of Dalriada', and who he thinks may have provided the germ for the later legend, was killed at the battle of the Miathi, which has been located variously at CouparAngus or at Kincardine O'Neill, but which may well have been fought further south in the district of the Ochils (Manau Gododdin).

ASSEMBLY'S COLLEGE, BELFAST.
See MacLeod, John.

AUCHENGIBBERT FARM, (Stewartry
of Kirkcudbright). *See* Simpson, Elspeth.

AUCHTERMUCHTY (Fife). *See* Serf;
Gillespie Church; Glas, John.

AUGUSTINE BRISTO CONGREGATIONAL CHURCH, EDINBURGH. *See* Aikman, John.

AVOCH (Kilcurdy). *See* Curitan.

BAILLIE, Lady Grisell (1). 1665–1746.
The Lady of Mellerstain whose epitaph claims for her 'Good breeding, Good humour, Good sense' was born Grisell Hume, daughter to Sir Patrick Hume of Redbraes Castle in the Borders. He was a leading Covenanter and friend to Robert Baillie who was hanged, drawn and quartered for his supposed implication in the Ryehouse Plot against the life of King James. At the age of 12 Grisell carried a message from her father to Baillie in the Edinburgh Tolbooth prison. Later, but before she was 20, she hid her father, first at Redbraes, and then, for greater safety, in the vault below Polwarth Church. The story of her heroism has been told many times, most dramatically in Wilson's *Tales of the Borders*. As persecution intensified, the family escaped to Holland, joining the little group of exiles sheltering at the court of William of Orange. Here she met again young George Baillie of Jerviswoode, son of the executed Covenanter. With the accession of William to the British throne they were all free to return. Sir Patrick Hume became Chancellor of Scotland and was created Earl of Marchmont. Grisell married George Baillie and they commissioned William Adam to begin the building of what eventually became graceful Mellerstain House. Lady Grisell was of considerable talent and one of her poems 'Were na my heart light I wad die' finds a place in Scots anthologies.

BAILLIE, Lady Grisell (2). 1822–91.
Great-great-granddaughter of the Covenanting Grisell. Her father, George Baillie, lived simply on the Mellerstain estate. He married the daughter of Sir James Pringle of Stichel, a lady popularly known as 'the pocket Venus'. Of their large family of 11, Grisell, the youngest, who had inherited her mother's intense beauty, was the only one to remain unmarried. Although the title had by-passed her father she was raised to the rank of an earl's daughter. Her four sisters became the Marchioness of Breadalbane, Lady Aberdeen, Lady Polwarth and the Countess of Ashburnham

Lady Grisell Baillie (2), aet. 20

respectively. Lady Grisell cared for her parents in their later years and then lived with her two brothers at Dryburgh Abbey, an active member of the parish church and noted for her charity. On most days, it was said, she could be seen, accompanied by her brother Major Baillie, visiting some of the aged, sick or needy. When Dr Charteris began settlement work in the St Leonard's district of Edinburgh — which was later to develop into St Ninian's Mission Church and the Deaconess Hospital — he decided to revive the ancient Order of Deaconesses in the Church of Scotland. Because of her interest and her own good works in the Borders, Lady Grisell was invited, and consented, to become the first deaconess.

BALCHRYSTIE (Fife). One mile west of Colinsburgh, this tiny hamlet was the scene of the birth of the sect known as the Old Scots Independents, now long disbanded. In 1768 two Church of Scotland ministers, Robert Ferrier of Largo and James Smith of Newburn, adopted Independent or Congregationalist principles and left the Church. Influenced by John Glas† they erected a meeting place and became elders of the body which rejected a single paid minister or pastor. Eventually there were eight or nine congregations loosely linked in fellowship, the most interesting being those in Paisley who were known as the 'Pen Folk'. Their most notable elder was

David Dale† of the Candle Kirk in Glasgow. He took Ferrier to help him but they quarrelled and Ferrier became a Glassite.

BALDOVY (Montrose). *See* Melville, Andrew.

BALFOUR, James, of Denholm. *See* Abdie Kirk.

BALFOUR, John, of Burley. *See* Rosneath.

BALIOL, John. *See* Sweetheart Abbey.

BALL, Thomas Isaac. *See* Cumbrae.

BALLACHULISH. *See* Chinnery-Haldane.

BALMAGHIE CHURCH (Stewartry of Kirkcudbright). Three Covenanting martyrs lie in the graveyard — George Short and two of the same name, David Halliday — all shot within a few months of each other in 1685 by Grierson of Lag. Part of the doggerel inscription on the larger stone reads

> 'These were the causes, not to be forgot, why they by Lag so wickedly were shot.
> One name, one cause, one grave, one heaven do ty their souls to that one God eternally.'

The Galloway novelist, S. R. Crockett is buried here, and here the Rev. John Macmillan, founder of the Reformed Presbyterians, ministered until ejected in 1706.

BAMBURGH [Bebbanburgh]. *See* Aidan.

BANFF. *See* Simpson, Elspeth.

BANGOR (Ulster). *See* Paisley.

BANNATYNE, Colin Archibald. 1849–1920. Son of the Free Church minister at Oban, he was ordained to Culter Free Church in 1876. He was a disciple of the Rev. James Begg† and assumed his mantle as leader of the 'Constitutional Party'. In April 1900, a group of 20 conservative ministers of the Free Church met at Achnasheen and resolved to remain outside the union with the United Presbyterians which now seemed inevitable. Bannatyne became a leading figure in the tug-of-war between the majority party, who had with the union become the United Free Church, and his minority who claimed to be the true remnant, loyal to the original concepts of the Disruption, and who claimed property and funds. At first their claim was rejected by the Scottish Courts but the House of Lords upheld it by their judgement of August 1904. In the end, however, the 'constitutionalists' had to be content with the number of churches etc. which were deemed sufficient for their membership. Bannatyne was the first Moderator of the Free Church after the split and in 1905 became Professor of Church History in New College. When the New College premises were handed back to the U.F. professors he and his colleagues were housed where their successors remain today — in the former offices of the Free Church on the Mound. He was appointed Moderator a second time in 1906 and held his Church History chair until the year of his death.

BARBOURS OF BONSKEID. *See* Drummond, Henry.

BARCLAY, John. 1736–98. Founder of the Berean sect at Fettercairn, which eventually spread to London, Bristol, Edinburgh and five or six other towns. The name was taken from Acts 17 where the Christians at Berea 'received the Word with all readiness of mind and searched the scriptures daily'. Born at Muthill, Barclay studied at St Andrews, attracted to Professor Campbell's 'enlightened' views, as opposed to those of Professor Tullideph, the 'Moderate' leader. Assistant at Errol he was dismissed, perhaps because the minister had married Tullideph's daughter. Later, assistant to Rev. Antony Dow, the aged minister of Fettercairn, where he began to attract large crowds to services, his doctrine became suspect and on Dow's death he was prohibited by the Presbytery (whose members he had called 'swine') from preaching within the parish. Although the people were for Barclay, Mr Foote of Eskdalemuir, with only 3 votes, was imposed on them. When refused a certificate of character, Barclay appealed to the Assembly, where he was represented at the Bar by James Boswell, advocate, the famous companion of Dr Johnson. By the end of the same year (1773) we find him leading an independent church of Bereans

in Edinburgh — at first in St Andrew Chapel at the foot of Carrubbers Close and later in Magdalen Chapel†. His Fettercairn followers had already with remarkable speed built for him a large barn-like meeting-house at Sauchieburn cross-roads just outside the boundary. Although they 'called' him as minister and he seems to have been there a few weeks, he preferred Edinburgh and left with them James McRae, a young schoolmaster. The people seem to have resented his not staying with them for they did not subscribe to his publications (it may be they could not read) and his name does not appear on the tablet which still stands on the wall of what is now a farm shed but was once the church of a large congregation. Barclay had not been ordained in the Church of Scotland and was now 'set apart' by Independent ministers at Newcastle for his Edinburgh work — which was to be life-long except for a two year visit to the south to set up churches in London, Bristol and elsewhere. Because of extreme poverty he was never able to revisit his churches in England but kept in touch with the Scots Bereans at Dundee, Arbroath, Stirling, Crieff and Glasgow by long walking tours. He is buried in the Old Calton graveyard, with his successor in the Edinburgh church, James Donaldson, beside him. The latter had previously been pastor in Dundee in a hall off the Overgate. Their last Edinburgh pastor was Daniel Hollis, ordained 1839. We finally hear of them in 1843 with ministers still in Edinburgh, Glasgow, Dundee and Laurencekirk, but none in England. Bereans held that 'assurance was of the essence of faith', did not use the word 'sacrament' nor consecrate the elements at Communion, and had a type of Independent government. The only tenet peculiar to Barclay and his followers was the view that Old Testament prophecies and the psalms referred exclusively to Christ and should not be applied to ourselves. He termed the usual commentaries 'a pack of lies' and published his own translations of psalms with commentaries, and some spiritual poems. Up to about 1940 Montrose Congregationalists held an annual service at the old Sauchieburn meetinghouse.

BARCLAY, Robert, of Ury. 1648–90.

Friend of George Fox and William Penn, Barclay was the aristocrat, scholar and apologist among the early Quakers. His major work, *Apology for the True Christian Divinity* became the standard text-book and authority for belief and practice of the Society of Friends for two centuries. He was a direct descendant of James I; his mother, Catherine Gordon, was cousin to Charles I and Robert was born and brought up at her home, Gordonstoun in Moray. His father, David Barclay, had been colonel in the Covenanting army in the Civil War but, repelled by the bickering and bloodshed, had given up politics before the Restoration. He was, however, imprisoned in Edinburgh castle because he had held office under the Commonwealth, and here he was converted to Quakerism by his cell-mate, John Swinton, ancestor of Walter Scott. Young Robert Barclay, who had been educated in the Reformed tradition in schools in Morayshire and in the Catholic tradition at the Scots College, Paris, where his uncle was Rector, also became a Friend and at the first Quaker wedding in Aberdeen (1670) married Christian Molleson. Father and son developed their recently acquired estate at Ury near Stonehaven in the intervals between frequent imprisonment and persecution. Their family connections and their Quaker pacificism shielded them from the fiercest of the persecutions which the Covenanters were suffering. David Barclay personally

Ury Mansion House, home of Robert Barclay (now demolished)

pleaded with Charles II for himself and for other Friends. Robert found an ally on the continent in his relative the Princess Palatine who secured for the Quakers the good offices of Prince Rupert. When in London Robert attended the Court and became friendly with the Duke of York, later James II and VII. He had no love of Romanism but his schooling under his uncle at the Scots College led him to understand James, whose Toleration Acts he believed were perfectly sincere. On the accession of King William, Barclay retired to Ury. His father David, who had built the house and also a meeting-house and had seen the estate raised to a barony, had died in 1685. Robert was appointed governor of the East Jersey colonial scheme in 1682 and although he never visited his colony he was able to help some of the Covenanting prisoners in Dunnottar Castle by having them sent across as colonists. He died at the early age of 42 and was buried in the mausoleum at Ury which still exists although the house and the meeting-house are long since demolished. Through his three sons and four daughters Robert Barclay was progenitor of a number of famous people: Elizabeth Fry, Francis Galton, William Forster (of the 1870 Education Act), and the powerful Barclay's Bank.

BARNARD CASTLE (Yorkshire). *See* Sweetheart Abbey.

BARNTON HOUSE, EDINBURGH. *See* Maxwell, Willielma.

BARONY CHURCH, GLASGOW. *See* Macleod, Norman.

BARRY (Angus). *See* Kirk, John.

BEATON [Bethune], **David**. *c.* 1494–1546. The Cardinal, the most brilliant of a trio of ecclesiastical statesmen from the same Fife family. See the notes below for his uncle James and his nephew James — all three were archbishops. David Beaton was educated at St Andrews, Glasgow and Paris; became Bishop of Mirepoix in France in 1537, created cardinal the following year and succeeded his uncle as Archbishop of St Andrews in 1539. Personally he seems to have been a man of piety although like many of his contemporaries he flouted his vow of celibacy;

politically he stood for Scottish independence against England's threat of annexation by Henry VIII. Beaton genuinely loved the Church of the old order as he had known it and so he culpably shut his eyes to its failings and considered it part of his duty (as technically it was) to show the utmost severity to all who might bring about its downfall. To achieve this he spared not the sword, and he perished by it.

BEATON [Bethune], **James** (1). d. 1539. Uncle of the above. Archbishop of Glasgow, then of St Andrews. Chancellor of Scotland, regent to the young James V. A milder ecclesiastic than his nephew and perhaps a greater statesman. He, too, maintained the French alliance against the English party.

BEATON [Bethune] **James** (2). 1517–1603. Nephew of the Cardinal. Because of the Reformation he spent much of his life abroad in France where for many years he represented Scotland at the French court. He was held in respect by all parties and in 1598 was restored to his benefice as Archbishop of Glasgow to which he had originally been appointed in 1552.

BEAULY PRIORY (Inverness-shire). Beauly (Beau Lieu or Bellus Locus = a lovely spot) with Ardchattan† and Pluscarden† are the only three priories of the Valliscaulian order outside France, where it originated as an offshoot of the Carthusians and the Cistercians which had been, in their turn, offshoots of the Benedictines. As the original orders tended to become slacker or more worldly, the monastic movement produced splinter groups forming new orders with tighter rules and stricter discipline. The Valliscaulians were one such, founded by a lay brother called Viard, who, toward the end of the twelfth century left his Carthusian monastery to seek greater solitude and a more devout life in the Val des Choux (Kail Glen). The order was recognized by the Pope in 1206 but restricted to some 20 houses in France and these three in Scotland, all founded in 1230. The ruins at Beauly are still impressive, with a very long, narrow church, no separation between chancel and nave, following the simplicity of the early Cistercian houses. In this order each unit was termed a Priory

under a Prior, not as in other orders where a Prior was deputy to an Abbot and the building was an Abbey. The last Prior was Robert Reid†, also Abbot of Kinloss and Bishop of Orkney. His arms are still on the west front which he rebuilt on the very eve of the Reformation. His nephew, Walter, joined the new movement and became the first Commendator of Beauly.

BEGG, James. 1808–83. Son of a Lanarkshire manse; graduated Glasgow; assistant North Leith and served in Lady Glenorchy's Chapel. After brief ministries at Maxwelltown and Paisley he became minister at Liberton, then a village beyond the Edinburgh boundary. As one of the leaders of the 'Evangelical Party' he relinquished his parish at the disruption of 1843 and became first minister of Newington Free Church (later St Paul's, Newington). Dr Begg entered warmly into all the controversies of his day: education, the new Higher Criticism and the relations between Church and State. He headed the 'Constitutional Party' in the Free Church which resisted the 'voluntaries' who desired a clean break between Church and State. He is remembered best for his interest in better housing for the working people; he set up the Edinburgh Co-operative Building Company which built tenement homes, advanced for their day and available on deferred terms, known generally to Edinburgh citizens as 'Begg's Buildings'. *See also* Robertson Smith, William.

BELLSHILL. *See* Gillespie Church.

BIGGAR, John. *See* Sciennes.

BIRR (Synod of). *See* Adamnan.

BLAIRLOGIE (Stirlingshire). *See* Gillespie Church.

BLAIRS COLLEGE (Kincardineshire). In 1829 the Roman Catholic seminary at Aquhorties which had housed the students for the priesthood since the closing of the remote Banffshire College at Scalan† moved to new and much larger premises at Blairs, near Aberdeen, where they were joined by students from the Highland College at Lismore. The property was the gift of John Menzies, last Laird of Pitfodels, of an ancient Catholic family. In 1827 he gifted his remaining estate, Blairs, for a Catholic seminary and for a time stayed in part of the premises and kept in close touch with the college. This apparently did not work out well and so he retired to live in Edinburgh until his death in 1843. The first rector was John Sharp, who held office for 18 years and who had been a student and later a Professor at Scalan. In the rectorship of Aeneas Chisholm (1890–9), later Bishop of Aberdeen and one of the outstanding Catholics of the century, a completely new set of buildings were erected, extensive and efficient if not architecturally prepossessing. The need for a worthy church for the college was met by the generosity of an English priest who had little connection with Scottish Catholicism — Mons. James Lennon who had known Blairs through his friendship with Scots students at Douai. He is buried beside the church which he gifted.

BLANC, Hippolyte. *See* Paisley.

BLANE. d. *c.* 590. There is a tradition that St Catan, coming to Bute to evangelize with his sister Eartha, in order that a 'coeducational' or dual community such as was not uncommon in the Celtic Church might be established, discovered that she was pregnant by some unknown man. In his anger he set her to sea in an oarless boat which drifted across the channel to Ulster where her son, Blane, was safely delivered. Growing up he became a respected monk who, in his turn, travelled to Bute where he became successor to his uncle, Catan, at the small community on Kilchattan Bay called Kingarth. Later Blane evangelized on the mainland — Blanefield (Campsie Hills), Kirkblane and Kilblane (Dumfriesshire), Petblain (Aberdeenshire) and other such names commemorate him. Eventually, it is said, he built the first church where Dunblane Cathedral now stands and he died there. Such biographies of Celtic saints should always be received with caution; they are built up from the mediaeval *Vitae*, or 'lives' which were read in the refectory while the monks ate and were light reading rather than serious history. Many place names may have originated centuries after the date of the saint because of an oratory or chapel containing a relic, or simply dedicated to him. On the other

hand, saints' names are not merely invented; there was a Celtic missionary called Blane and the chances are that he evangelized in the districts where his name is most remembered.

BLANEFIELD. *See* Blane.

BLANTYRE (Lanarkshire). *See* Livingstone, David.

BOECE, Hector. *See* Elphinstone, William.

BOISIL. *See* Cuthbert.

BONIFACE [Bonifacius]. *See* Curitan.

BONNINGTON MILL. *See* Hickhorngill, Edward.

BOSTON, Thomas. *See* Ettrick Kirk.

BOSTON, Thomas, the Younger. *See* Gillespie Church.

deBOTHWELL, Richard. d. 1470. Of the estate of Hallbank, near Dunfermline; became monk at the Abbey, Sacristan from 1423 and Abbot 1445–70. While Sacristan at Dunfermline he was also Abbot of Paisley† and unsuccessful candidate for the Priory of Urquhart. Viewing the west front and north-west corner of the Abbey from the Glen one is struck by the beauty of the porch — an important feature of the mediaeval building as certain marriages and the baptisms would be performed there — and by a distinct but irregular change in the colour of the stonework in the great west wall. Both features are due to deBothwell, who repaired and partly reconstructed the west end of the nave. Impressed by the solidity of mediaeval buildings, the observer today may not realise that in days before scientific maintenance, adequate heating and proper ventilation, such buildings deteriorated rapidly and in the period between the twelfth century and the Reformation several had to be almost completely rebuilt; some towers collapsed, and walls, like that which troubled Abbot deBothwell, began to bulge dangerously. It is perhaps a mercy that the good Abbot, who gave himself so generously to his beloved building, could have had no foreknowledge that in just over a century the choir would be allowed to fall into ruins, and the nave which he had beautified would be ceiled and lofted with galleries to serve as the Protestant parish church. He was also responsible for moving the grammar school up into the burgh, to a site in Queen Anne Street still marked by stones set into the modern post-office building. When the only available education was in monastic schools the presence of numbers of boys from the burghs conflicted with the peace and quiet necessary to monastic cloisters, and schools, such as Dunfermline, were often removed outwith the precincts. One or more monks continued to act as schoolmasters and the Abbey retained its authority. At a time when nepotism and corruption were sapping the spiritual energy of the Church it is good to find men like deBothwell whose integrity and devotion are beyond question. Among other bequests he left 'four merks a year for the upkeep of a wax candle of one pound weight at the high altar near the picture of St. Margaret . . . to burn during the divine office . . .' Requiescat in pace!

BRANDSBUTT PICTISH STONE (Aberdeenshire). *See* Inverurie.

BRECHIN. *See* Guthrie. Thomas: Willison, John.

BRIDE [Brigit, Bridget, or Brighde]. There are several Brides or Bridgets — the historical, the traditional and the legendary figures. (*a*) The legendary, pre-Christian, Celtic Brigit gave her name to the tribe Brigantes as their tutelary goddess. She was the Gaelic Minerva, a principal figure in the legends of the Tuatha De Danaan and the Firbolgs. (*b*) The historical St Bridget of Kildare, *c*. 452–524, born to the Christian slave of a pagan master, Dubthach, near Kildare where later she built a monastery. In Ireland she is set in honour beside Patrick and Columcille and the tradition (certainly untrue) is that they lie together under a massive boulder beside Downpatrick Cathedral. (*c*) The traditional Bride or Bridget is largely a confluence of the two above together with stories from other female saints, who may or may not have borne the same name. It is fairly certain that the foundress of Kildare never came to Scotland, yet place-names abound with forms like Kilbride, Panbride, Bridekirk and even Pitlumbertie (homestead of the hamlet of Bride). Significantly the frequency of

such names is greatest in Wigtownshire and round the Solway, but it is in Gaelic Scotland that the mention of Bride raises a tear, or a song, or an oft-repeated story. Particularly in those islands where centuries of Protestantism have not erased the traditions, she is 'Muime Chriosd', foster-mother to the infant Jesus, or she is Mary of the Gael, or Bride, the calm one of the smooth, white palms and the clustering, gold-brown hair. The least fulsome and most loving tribute is from the Book of Lismore — 'She was abstinent, she was innocent, she was prayerful, she was patient, she was glad in God's commandments, she was firm, she was humble, she was forgiving, she was loving, she was a consecrated casket for keeping Christ's Body and His Blood, she was a temple of God. Her heart and her mind were a throne of rest for the Holy Ghost.' Kildare became a famous co-educational monastery, with inmates of both sexes, but this was probably after Bridget's day. In Ireland little rush crosses, especially the design known as the three legged triskele, are woven on her anniversary, February 1st, which is traditionally the first day of Spring. *See also* Abernethy.

BRIDGE OF WEIR (Renfrewshire). *See* Quarrier, William.

BRIGHTON STREET E. U. CHAPEL, EDINBURGH. *See* Morison, James.

BRODIE OF BRODIE. *See* Rose, Hugh.

BROWN, John. 1722–87. Usually termed 'of Haddington' to distinguish him from several illustrious relatives, especially his great-grandson, the author of *Rab and His Friends*. Born at Carpow, near Abernethy, he was the nearest the Secession ever possessed to an infant prodigy, for he was entirely self-educated, learned the three classical languages to great depth and eight other tongues without tutor or grammar book by a process of applied logic, using only a copy of the scripture in the unknown tongue. He became a professor without ever having been at a university, His power over language was so great that it was seriously asserted that he was taught by the devil, and it is to the discredit of his minister, Alex. Moncrieff†, that he believed and encouraged this charge. Had

c

the dates been a half-century earlier, it is likely that Moncrieff would have had him burned as a witch. As it was he put every obstacle in the way of the lad who wanted to be a minister, and years later disciplined his members for going to hear Brown preach. Young Brown left Abernethy, never to return, and became in turn a packman in Fife, temporary soldier on the government side in the '45 (although he had no more military duty than helping to protect Edinburgh castle), and school-master at Gairney Bridge†. In the Seces-sion dispute he took the Burgher side and often tramped to Dunfermline to hear Ralph Erskine. The Associate Synod accepted him as a student and in the vacations he continued, as was customary, to teach. Ordained to Haddington in 1751 he remained there all his life with a stipend never greater than £50 a year. His abilities were such that in just over two years he was Moderator of the supreme court of his denomination, and later became its per-manent Principal Clerk, a post he retained without remuneration until his death. He was the natural choice as professor to the Burgher students, a post he held along with his pastoral charge; the students came to lodge in Haddington and attended lectures in his manse. Not only did Brown fulfil each office with devoted care but began the voluminous writings for which he is remembered. In this sense he might well be termed the William Barclay of his day: both men decided to devote their scholarship to popular writing which would open the scriptures to a wide circle of readers; both have produced a pro-digious amount of literary material while holding down full-time posts with accep-tance. Brown is remembered today for his two-volume *Dictionary of the Bible* (1769) and the *Self-interpreting Bible* (1778) of which 26 editions were issued. He also wrote on the psalms, on prophecy, on the history of the Church, on various Secession disputes and a mass of devotional material and pamphlets. He aimed at what he termed 'universal scholarship', but before the end admitted that it was impossible to become an authority on all aspects of religion. When he died he had been minister at Haddington for 36 years and Divinity Professor for 20.

BROWNE, Gilbert. *See* Sweetheart Abbey.

BROWNE, Robert. *fl.* 1580. Fleeing from England because of Independent or Con-gregationalist views of the Church, Browne first sheltereed in France, then came to Scotland. He landed at Dundee in 1583 and proceeded the following year to Edin-burgh. Andrew Melville† at St Andrews gave him some encouragement but he faced persecution from the Kirk and within a short time left to return to England. His influence, however, continued, and forty years later the King and Council were convinced that 'Brownism' was infecting Edinburgh.

BRUCE, Michael. 1746–67. Son of a cottage weaver of Kinnesswood, near Kinross, Michael was allowed by the local laird free schooling along with his own family and other village boys. He went up to Edinburgh University, walking to the ferry and returning each 'Meal Monday' to renew his supply of meal and eggs. He lodged in the Grassmarket with John Logan, a divinity student. On completing Arts he went in the short term to study divinity at the Seceders college in Kinross, following the usual practice of teaching during the rest of the year. He was a rather unsuccessful schoolmaster at Gairney-bridge and soon transferred to Forest Mill. On the journey to the latter place his horse

Birthplace of Michael Bruce, Kinnesswood

An incised bull-stone from Burghead

stumbled and he fell into the Black Devon, catching the chill which developed into 'the wasting' which caused his death at the early age of 21. It was known locally that he had written several poems, including some 'sacred songs' which had been sung at choir practice in Portmoak to prevent misuse of the sacred words of the psalms. When his former fellow-student John Logan called at the Bruce cottage saying that he desired to publish Michael's poems he was given all the MSS. After much delay and frustration the family were sent a slim volume and Logan claimed most of the songs and poems as his own. For well over a century the paraphrases in question were attributed to Logan, although a body of opinion, led by Dr Baird, Principal of Edinburgh University, had always protested that they had been plagiarised. Although the paraphrases or gospel sonnets are now generally recognized as from Bruce there is still uncertainty about some poems. Two of the poems are still worthwhile, 'Lochleven' and 'To a Cuckoo', but neither shows great originality. Of the paraphrases the greatest are 11, 18, 23 and the popular second paraphrase which represents Bruce's emendation of Doddridge's original version.

BRUIDE macDERILE. *See* Curitan.

BUCHANAN, George. *See* Winzet, Ninian.

BUCHANAN, Thomas. *See* Erskine, R.

BUCHANITES. *See* Innes, Andrew; Simpson, Elspeth.

BUDGE, John. *See* Keiss.

BURGHEAD (Moray). Well-designed example of early nineteenth century town planning on a magnificent headland site on the Moray Firth. Unfortunately the plans cut through, although they did not completely destroy, the best example we have in Scotland of a Pictish fort. At least eight stones with incised bulls, all very fierce and warlike, have been found nearby and the inference is that the fort may have been the headquarters of a Pictish 'Bull Tribe'. All the bull stones, except one rather poor specimen, have been removed to museums in London, Edinburgh and Elgin, but there are good casts, with other interesting local relics, in the harbourmaster's office. A so-called Roman well nearby (AM) may have been an early Christian baptismal tank; dating from the Dark Ages it may have been successor to the original well which supplied the Pictish fort. The place for the annual 'Burning of the Clavie' may be seen — a pagan festival which has survived to the present day but is now in danger of being discontinued.

BURNS, Robert (Free Church minister). *See* Burns, William C.

BURNS, Robert (poet). *See* Innes, Andrew; Geddes, John.

BURNS, Thomas. *See* Maxwell, Willielma.

BURNS, William C. 1815–68. Born in the manse at Dun (Angus), and brought up in Kilsyth manse to which the family had moved, Burns was a strange, unsettled member of the extreme Evangelical Party in the Church of Scotland and, after 1843, in the Free Church. In an earlier generation he would have been happy touring the country with James Haldane†; a later one would probably have found him with the Pentecostals. As it was, after Divinity studies at Glasgow and Aberdeen, he found satisfaction, not in the steady ministry of a parish, but in organizing revival campaigns: in his father's parish where memories of the great revival of the previous century lingered; in Dundee, where McCheyne left him in charge of St Peter's while he was in the Holy Land; in Aberdeen, where the Presbytery set up a committee to investigate the happenings but received a favourable report; in Perth, Breadalbane, etc. His Scottish campaigns resulted in much real revival (although we rely on the uncritical biography by his brother) but abroad he met with much opposition and derision. In Newcastle he was indiscreet in selecting the cattle market for his meeting and was pelted with dung; in Ireland he scarcely escaped from the mob with his life. His Dublin host, Dr W. B. Kilpatrick of Mary's Abbey Church, comments that 'his addresses failed to make much impression on our Presbyterian people' and that he would have been better to prepare his sermons more carefully instead of blaming the people for not listening. On occasions he was both spectacular and persistent, as when the Edinburgh and Glasgow Railway began to run Sunday trains. He was seen standing outside Haymarket Station on a large stone before the first train started at 7 a.m. singing the psalm

> 'Horror took hold on me because
> Ill men Thy law forsook . . .'

. . . and two hours after the last train at 6 p.m. he was still there with a large crowd round him. Perhaps he realized that even in the Free Church there was little scope for itinerant evangelists, for in 1844 he left to engage in a 'missionary tour' of Upper Canada. The proceedings and papers of the United Synod of the Presbyterians in Canada reveal that this was by no means a tour to convert heathen to Christianity; rather, it was a carefully designed plan by his uncle, Dr Robert Burns, and some Free Church leaders to convert Canadian Presbyterians from their former unity and harmony to a disruption on the lines of that in their home country. 'Where-ever Burns travelled, the Disruption followed' (J. S. Moir, *The Cross in Canada*, Toronto 1966) was written of the uncle but applied also to the nephew. He went up the Ottawa River to Bytown (now Ottawa) and down the line of the Rideau Canal, and little out-back villages like Perth, Lanark and Smith's Falls found themselves saddled with two rival Presbyterian groups. It was not so much a revival in Canada as a puritan swing — after the Free Church got going in Glengarry County 'Bagpipes and fiddles were cast into the fire; balls, merry-making and festivals given up'. Perhaps it is shameful but today the same district boasts at least one very fine girls' pipe-band and a rollicking Highland games. On his return to Scotland, Burns turned to the rapidly expanding foreign mission field; in 1847 he was ordained in Sunderland as first missionary of the English Presbyterian Church to China, where over 50 missionaries had poured in since Britain forced open the ports. Burns was a good linguist and the pioneer Robert Morrison had left a translation of the scriptures, yet his work in China was not notable; the various fields were over-harvested by competing societies. For the rest of his life, 16 years, he only returned home once. He worked up and down the China coast, connected at various times with Canton, Nanking and Peking, but most at home in the island of Amoy where his best work was done. There is no record of Burns performing a baptism either at home or abroad and he made clear to the committee appointing him to China that he desired ordination only to preach and not to celebrate sacraments. His views on ministerial orders are not clear but apparently he saw himself as holding the primitive office of evangelist but not of presbyter.

CABRACH (Banffshire). *See* Morison, James; Macdonald, Hugh.

CAINNECH. *See* Kenneth.

CAIRD, John. 1820–98. Born at Greenock, Caird began in his father's engineering works, but later entered Glasgow University where he distinguished himself in divinity. In 1845 he began his ministry at Newton-on-Ayr, at a time when the Disruption had denuded the Church of Scotland of so many of its best men. Within a year he was called to Lady Yester's, Edinburgh, where his preaching attracted large crowds and helped to show that the 'auld kirk' was not yet dead. Overworked and not too happy in this city parish Caird accepted a call to the rural charge of Errol in the Carse of Gowrie. He avoided being dragged in to the controversial politics of the time and in a quieter way was as successful at Errol as in the city. He established a model Industrial School before he left in 1857 for Park Church, Glasgow. In the same year, Queen Victoria, who had been impressed by his preaching at Crathie, appointed him one of her chaplains. Later he was called to the chair of divinity at Glasgow and in 1873 appointed Principal of the University. At a time when ministers who did not 'come out' at the Disruption suffered much opprobrium, Caird, and a small band of similarly talented men, quietly but steadily restored public respect for the Established Church. Through his influence on the divinity students of all communions who heard his University sermons, preached four times each term to a packed Bute Hall, he did much to pave the way for the ecumenical movement of the following century. His brother Edward expounded the idealism of Hegel as Professor of Moral Philosophy in Glasgow (1866–94) and later was Master of Balliol. *See also* Struthers, J. P.

CAIRNEYHILL (Fife). *See* Gillespie, Thomas.

CAIRNS, John. 1818–92. Principal Cairns personifies the life and faith of the United Presbyterian Church — as the 'New Lichts' among the Seceders were called after Burghers and Anti-burghers had united with the Relief. Born of humble Berwickshire farm stock he was the typical 'lad o' pairts' who distinguished himself at Edinburgh by taking all before him in Classics, Logic and Moral Philosophy, where he had as mentors Sir Wm Hamilton and John Wilson (Christopher North). After passing through the Secession Divinity Hall he began a long ministry at Berwick, first at Golden Square, then moving to a new church at Wallace Green, where he maintained the ideals of the Seceding ministry: unadorned services with lengthy exegetical sermons unread, backed by regular pastoral visitation. It was said he refused two professorships and the offer of principalship of Edinburgh University. He played a full part in the higher courts of his denomination, arguing always for 'Voluntarism', the separation of Church from State, and led the party which pressed for disestablishment of the Church of Scotland. He convened the committee for union with the Free Church 30 years before it became possible and he conceived the idea of a 'Declaratory Act' to soften the rigidity of the Westminster Confession. In 1867 he accepted the chair of Apologetics in the U. P. Hall or college. At the time such professors acted only for some two months in the summer and so could retain their charges, but in 1875 the Synod decided to bring their college into line with other denominations and he became full-time in Edinburgh, severing his connection with Berwick. This saved him a difficult decision; until then the Seceders in England remained U.P. and Britain was treated as one church with headquarters in Edinburgh. The congregations south of the Border now decided to unite with the English Presbyterians. Had Cairns remained at Wallace Green he would have become an English Free Church minister cut off from his Scottish brethren. The full circle has been accomplished since his day for in 1972 the same congregation petitioned the General Assembly of the Church of Scotland to be admitted. So Cairns' own church has eventually become part of that which he sought so hard to destroy. In 1872 he was Moderator of the U.P. Synod and in 1879 appointed Principal of their college in the Synod Hall, Castle Terrace — later to become a cinema specializing in horror films, then a site for a projected opera house. Late in life his interest in languages revived while his interest in apologetics declined. After he was 60 he learned Arabic, Assyrian, Dutch and Spanish while others were in controversy over Darwin and evolution; it might be said, not unkindly, that scholarship had passed him by. He died at his house in Spence Street and after a great service in the Synod Hall, was buried in Echobank Cemetery. The influence of the Cairns family has long continued to be felt in Scottish Church life, first through Principal Cairns' nephews, David and William. The former became Professor and later Principal in Aberdeen U. F. College while the latter played a major role in the preparation of the *Revised Church Hymnary*. David's son, another David, subsequently held the chair of Practical Theology in his father's old college from 1947 to 1972.

CALDWELL, John. *fl.* 1765. Founder of the Moravian Mission in Ayrshire. The Moravian Church, known also as the Unitas Fratrum, or Brethren (but distinguish from modern 'Brethren') originated in Bohemia before the Reformation from groups of pious Christians who met for prayer. They did not rebel against the doctrines or ceremonies of the mediaeval church but laid little stress on ritual and refused to dispute about dogma. At the Reformation they organized themselves into the Church of the Brethren. Their leader, John Amos Comenius (1592–1672) was one of the outstanding educationists of all time and the sect has always been interested in founding schools. In the eighteenth century the German Count Zinzerndorff gave new strength to the movement and they became pioneers in missionary work, not only in the New World but in Britain and Ireland. John Wesley was greatly influenced by them and one of his followers, John Cennick, who had become a Moravian, preached widely in Ireland where several settlements were set up after the pattern of Zinzerndorff's original at Herrnhut. The community at Gracehill, near Ballymena, is still active, with its church, school, lay sisters' and brothers' houses clustered round the village. It was from this centre that Caldwell, of Ayrshire stock and a convert of Cennick, set up a community in Ayr in

1765. At first it was regarded only as a preaching station but in 1778, after a visit by the Moravian Bishop de Watteville it became a regular church. A little chapel was erected in Mill Vennel, 'a small, gabled structure with square windows', with a manse on one side and a girls' school on the other. The movement spread until it had preaching stations or churches at Irvine, Tarbolton, Dumfries, Annan, Kilsyth, Kilmarnock, Glasgow, Edinburgh and a few other places, but the growth did not last. Part of Moravian doctrine was to accept the Christian work of any denomination: it was Zinzerndorff himself who had coined the word 'oecumenical' and his missionaries would readily recommend their converts to join the Church of Scotland or any local church. Around Ayr, the movement persisted into the present century; services were discontinued when, in 1916, the last minister, the Rev. Norman Farquhar Orr sought admission to the Church of Scotland. He was a man of academic distinction typical of the Moravians. Educated at the school at Fulneck, he became minister at Stanley (1918), Wanlockhead (1924) and later served the Irish Presbyterian Church. The old burial ground of the Ayr church had the little daughter of one John Montgomery as its first inmate. He had come to Ayr in 1771 to help John Caldwell and was stationed in Irvine where his son James was born. In 1776 the Montgomerys moved to Gracehill, so James used later to say he 'narrowly escaped being an Irishman'. He became, of course, the great hymn-writer — 'Hail to the Lord's Anointed', 'Angels from the Realms of Glory' etc., while Cennick was author of 'Lo, He comes . . .', 'Children of the Heavenly King' and other popular hymns.

CAMBUSLANG (Lanarkshire). The year 1742 saw remarkable religious revivals in central Scotland at Cambuslang and Kilsyth. In the former parish William McCulloch had ministered without notable success for over 10 years when in the spring of 1742 there came quite suddenly what was known as 'The Awakening'. Crowds estimated at several thousands came from a wide district to hear sermons preached almost every day of the week at 'the preaching braes'. Unprecedented for the period, the Sacrament was repeated twice in the year. The minister was assisted in the revival by his neighbours, by other evangelically minded brethren from further afield such as Willison† of Dundee and Gillespie† of Carnock, and by the London Anglican evangelist George Whitefield†. The latter took part and preached at both Communion seasons, but he was not responsible for 'The Awakening' which was already in progress before he came north. The scene of the 'Cambuslang Wark', as it came to be known, was a 'green brae on the east side of a deep ravine near the church, scooped out by nature in the form of an amphitheatre' (*New Statistical Account*). The Rev. John Robe of Kilsyth, who assisted McCulloch at the great tent meetings, soon found a similar revival was taking place in his parish. The crowds at Kilsyth do not seem to have been so great, but the form was the same: the first signs followed a series of sermons on 'Regeneration' and 'The New Birth' by the minister, then the eloquence of Whitefield, Willison and other preachers increased the size of the crowds. In both cases there were instances of extreme psychological disturbance and emotion. After some months of intense fervour the number of cases of conversion steadily fell and attendances at services decreased, although for some years they remained higher than they had been before 'The Awakening'. The Seceders, who had first brought Whitefield north and had hoped to keep him to themselves, wrote and preached vehemently against the revivals which were centred on the parish churches and tended to divert people back from the Secession to the national Church. There were, of course, charges of excessive emotion and of backsliding, some of which appear to be justified, and upon these cases the Seceders fell in unChristian denunciation.

CAMBUSKENNETH ABBEY. *See* Foret, Thomas.

CAMBUSNETHAN (Lanarkshire). *See* Renwick, James.

CAMELON (Falkirk). *See* Arthur.

CAMPBELL, John (lay preacher). *See* Haldane, Robert and James.

CAMPBELL, John McLeod. 1800–72. Brought up in Kilninver Manse, Argyll, he was cousin to Norman Macleod†. Educated at Glasgow University he competed against Edward Irving† for the charge of the Scots Church, Hatton Garden. He was ordained to Row (or Rhu) in 1825. He was one of the first, and the most able of those who struggled to break the bonds of a Calvinist interpretation of the doctrine of Salvation, preaching a universal Atonement and a need for the 'assurance of salvation'. His magnum opus, *The Nature of the Atonement* appeared in 1855. Its profundity of thought is accompanied by much obscurity of language. He is the Abelard of Scottish thinkers on the Atonement and no subsequent theologian could afford to neglect him. Deposed in 1831, he was content to preach for some years in a small meeting house in Glasgow. When his health began to fail he retired to Rosneath† where he spent his last years in a house built for him by his consistent friend and protector, Thomas Erskine of Linlathen†.

CAMPSIE (Stirlingshire). *See* Lee, Robert.

CANONGATE KIRK, EDINBURGH. Originally built to serve the independent burgh of Canongate, it has the dubious honour of being erected at the command of James II and VII who wanted the nave of Holyrood Abbey for his exclusive use as the Chapel Royal, and also for the celebration of the mass which he was almost openly introducing. Since the Reformation the Canongate parishioners had used this part of the otherwise decaying abbey. When the king stopped them they complained that they could not worship at Lady Yester's, within Edinburgh royalty, 'as the ports were shut at the time of sermon', and so the new church was rather grudgingly built for them, and around it a large burying ground which was in time occupied by the bodies of many famous citizens, including Robert Fergusson (with epitaph by Burns), Adam Smith, Dugald Stewart, Provost Drummond, Horatius Bonar — and Dr Gregory of stomach-powder fame.

CARLISLE. *See* Cuthbert; Maxwell, Willielma; Tait, Archibald.

CARLYLE, Alexander. 1722–1808. For 37 years 'Jupiter' Carlyle ministered at

Inveresk and took a prominent part in the social life of Edinburgh in its golden age. He is always regarded as the epitome of the 'Moderate' minister, more worldly than spiritual, a High Tory (who even opposed the repeal of the Test Act by which Church of Scotland members resident in England had to become Episcopalians), a visitor to the playhouse, a moderate drinker of spirits and a sycophant who cultivated the acquaintance of lairds and gentry. Probably there were better sides to his character but his own autobiography does not reveal them. He has, however, his defenders who point to the conscientious performance of his parochial duties and to his enthusiasm — rare among moderate ministers — for the establishment of a Sabbath School.

CARLYLE, Thomas. *See* Erskine, Thomas; Irving, Edward.

CARNOCK (Fife). *See* Gillespie, Thomas.

CARPOW. *See* Abernethy.

CATAN. *See* Blane.

CAUSEWAYHEAD (Stirlingshire). *See* Logie Airth.

CENNICK, John. *See* Caldwell, John.

CEOLFRID. *See* Curitan.

CHALMERS, Thomas. 1780–1847. There are detailed biographies of Chalmers in abundance; contemporary *Reminiscences* by John Anderson and readable modern *Lives* by Hugh Watt and Adam Philip. Born at Anstruther, minister of one country parish (Kilmany) and two Glasgow charges, lecturer, while still very young, in mathematics and chemistry at St Andrews, later Professor of Moral Philosophy at the same university, Professor of Divinity at Edinburgh (where until recently one could see marks of the crush galleries which had to be erected in his lecture hall to hold the crowds) and finally, when the Disruption had torn him from his mother-church, Principal and Professor in New College when it really was new; D.D. Glasgow, D.C.L. Oxford, Chaplain to the King, not only first Moderator of the Free Church of Scotland but to a large extent its saint and guardian angel. Both the denomination he founded and the wider church has honoured and idolized him. The greatest man he had ever met, said Rainy, and Masson said exactly the same; Morley called him 'Mighty Chalmers', and he was variously described by his contemporaries and those who came after as 'Great Heart', 'The Incomparable Scot', 'The Moses of our Country', 'The Moral Engineer of Scotland'. Mr Gladstone remarked more moderately 'He does indeed seem to be an admirable man'. In this age, when the great nineteenth century heroes — Tennyson, Livingstone and even dear Grace Darling — fall before the modern debunker, it is remarkable that Dr Chalmers has so far escaped. His social work in Glasgow was monumental; his vision and energy in 'territorial' or mission charges revolutionized Scottish church life; in preaching and lecturing he was said to be superb; even those who find difficulty over immediate conversions must admit that something extraordinary in the religious line took place in Kilmany Manse. At his death the procession from his large mansion at the Churchhill corner in Edinburgh to the Grange Cemetery was the longest the city had ever seen and has never been equalled since.

CHAPEL OF GARIOCH (Aberdeenshire). *See* Inverurie.

CHAPEL OF THE CRAIGS (Banffshire).
See Hay, George.

CHARTERIS, Archibald Hamilton. *See*
Baillie, Lady Grisell (2).

CHERRY, Thomas. *See* Wesley, John.

CHINNERY-HALDANE, Alexander.
1842-1906. A Haldane of Gleneagles, he
was baptized James Robert Alexander, but
discarded the first two names, probably
because he had nothing in common with
his grandfather, James†, the famous evangelist who became a Baptist, or with his
great-uncle, Robert†, who was of like
persuasion. He married an Irish heiress,
daughter of the Rev. Sir Nicholas
Chinnery, and took the name Haldane-
Chinnery, which later in life he reversed to
Chinnery-Haldane, so making things difficult for those wanting to trace his curriculum vitae. His wife's parents were both
killed in the famous Abergele train disaster
and so he became extremely wealthy.
When acting as unpaid curate at All Saints,
Tollcross, Edinburgh, he lived in the
mansion Greenhill House and astonished
the city by maintaining one of the smartest
equipages in town. Edinburgh was alto-

gether too Presbyterian for him; neither his
wife nor he liked it, although the struggling,
working-class congregation of All Saints
appreciated both his ceaseless labours on
their behalf and his great generosity which
enabled them to survive when their parent
church, St John's Princes Street, had cut
them off for being 'Romish'. He found his
ideal ministry and home in the largely
Episcopalian district of Nether Lochaber
and Ballachulish, where he bought and
enlarged the mansion Alltshelloch (at the
north of the present bridge), and served
three small churches: St Bride's, on the
north side of Loch Leven, St John's on the
south, and St Mary's, Glencoe, which he
built and paid for himself. In 1883 he was
appointed Bishop of Argyll and the Isles,
and combined with some success the life of
a zealous prelate and a Scottish country-
gentleman. With Chinnery-Haldane the
'Catholicizing' of the Episcopal Church in
Scotland became complete. He was un-
compromising in what he considered 'the
True Church'; he rejected discussion with,
or approach to, Protestants of any type; he
refused to confirm catechumens unless they
had been baptized by a cleric 'in Apostolic
Succession'; he refused to officiate at the
marriage of a priest (his marriage had
taken place before he was priested), and he
expurgated his own library of all volumes
written by the reformers. His cousin, Lady
Monkwell, wrote of him 'The bishop is
quite a new variety'. He was so slow of
speech and action that he had to celebrate
mass with a watch in front of him. He was
a good pastor. He was instrumental in
building Bishop's House on Iona and he
revived the work in Cumbrae† at his own
expense.

CHISHOLM, Aeneas. *See* Blairs College.

CHRISTIE, William. *See* Palmer, T. F.

CITY TEMPLE, EDINBURGH. The
former Martyrs and St John's United Free
Church, George IV Bridge, was recently
acquired by the Elim Pentecostal Church
and reopened under the title of the City
Temple. The building was formerly the
principal place of worship of the Reformed
Presbyterians, successors to the Cameronians. On 22 May 1876, on their uniting with
the Free Church of Scotland, 37 ministers,

each with his elder, left the building and marched in procession to the Free Assembly Hall on the Mound. The congregation then became Martyrs Free Church — the title beloved by former R.P. congregations throughout Scotland — and on the greater union of 1929 it elected to maintain its freedom from any state connection and became part of the United Free Church (Continuing). The Elim Gospel movement spread in Britain as the result of visits of the American evangelist Pastor George Jeffreys, after the First World War. It maintains a type of strict Baptist order, fundamentalist in doctrine and revivalist and pentecostal in outlook. It now possesses units in most populous centres, strong in Belfast with 8 congregations, in Birmingham with 14 and in London with 21.

CLAPPERTON, Margaret. *See* Trail, Ann Agnes.

CLASHMAHEW (Wigtownshire). *See* Kirkmahoe.

CLERK'S LANE SECESSION CHURCH, KILMARNOCK. *See* Morison, James.

CLOSEBURN (Dumfriesshire). *See* Simpson, Elspeth.

COATES HALL, EDINBURGH, THEOLOGICAL COLLEGE. *See* Cumbrae; Dowden, John.

COATS MEMORIAL BAPTIST CHURCH, PAISLEY. *See* Paisley.

COCKLAW, Thomas. *See* Foret, Thomas.

COLDINGHAM PRIORY (Berwickshire). Edgar, fourth son of Malcolm Canmore and Saint Margaret, as ruler of Scotland (1097–1107), continued his mother's Durham connection by granting the Benedictine monks of Durham lands at Coldingham, *c.* 1098. At first probably just a 'grange' of the parent house, by the middle of next century it was a regular Priory served by Durham monks. Today only fragments of the cloister buildings remain but there is much good mediaeval work, some dating from the twelfth and thirteenth centuries, built into the present parish church. An upright female skeleton was revealed during restoration last century. As a Christian institution, however, Coldingham is much older than the medi-

aeval foundation date of 1147, for in his *Life of St Cuthbert* Bede introduces 'a nun called Aebbe, a real mother to the Lord's handmaids, in charge of the convent at Coldingham, honoured for piety and nobility alike, for she was King Oswiu's sister'. Ebba, one of a group of high-born, holy women of the Northumbrian Church, had been exiled with her royal brothers Oswald† and Oswy. On her return she founded a community, said to be 'coeducational', on St Abb's Head. She invited Cuthbert† to come to exhort the community and Bede draws a very human picture of the saint's visit. After Ebba's death in 683 the monastery was destroyed by fire. Traces of what may possibly have been her cell are pointed out near the headland.

COLERIDGE, Samuel Taylor. *See* Leighton, Robert.

COLIER, Thomas. *See* Gillespie Church.

COLINSBURGH (Fife). *See* Gillespie Church.

COLLEGE STREET CHURCH, EDINBURGH. *See* Gillespie Church.

COLMAN OF DROMORE. Sixth century. There are reputed to be over 100 saints of this name in the Irish Kalendars, but it is probably Colman or Colmoc of Druim Mór in Co. Down who is commemorated at Inchmahome (=innis (island) of Mo (my dear) Cholmaig). Little is known about him, but he was educated under St. Mochaoi (*see* under Kirkmahoe) at Nendrum on Island Mahee, a place which resembles Inchmahome†. Place names which may be connected are Kilmachalmaig (Bute), Kilmachumaig (Crinan), Portmahomack (Dornoch Firth) and a Capella Sancti Colmoci in Kirriemuir.

COLMAN OF LINDISFARNE. d. 674. Ab and third bishop of Lindisfarne. He came from Iona and led the defence of the Celtic Church against Wilfred at the Synod of Whitby (664). Colman resigned and returned to Iona but soon he and the Scots and Anglian monks who accompanied him sailed to the far west coast of Ireland where they founded the community of Inisbofin (the Isle of the White Cow). The *Felire* of Oengus records 'Colman, a praiseful bishop from the Isle of the White Cow . . . rested in the eightieth year of his age'. *See also* Ruthwell.

COLONSAY, Isle of. *See* Oronsay.

COLUMBA [Colum-cille] *c.* 521–597. 'This is the holy Presbyter, Columba, the Arch-priest (uasal-sagart) of the island of the Gael, Colum Cille, son of Fedlimid, son of Fergus Ceunfada, son of Conall Gulban, son of Niall of the Nine Hostages . . . Noble then was his kindred as regards the world. By right of birth he was fit to be chosen for the Kingship of Ireland, and it would have been offered to him had he not put it from himself for the sake of God.' So runs the *Irish Life of Columba*. The biographical facts are well known and reasonably well authenticated. It is the interpretations and additions which are often wide of the mark and produce the school-book portrait of the saint which is unreal. It is often suggested that he was an Irishman who deserted (or was forced to leave) his country to work in Scotland. In fact Dalriada (Argyll) was then a colony of Irishmen (Scots) with its king at Dunadd recently recognized as independent but still speaking a language (Gaelic) not understood by most of the people of Alba — which is modern Scotland. Iona was not nearly as remote from his first monastery at Derry as was Skellig Michael in the south of Ireland. Quite as important as his Scottish work was the chain of Irish monasteries (Derry, Durrow, Swords etc.) which introduced a new type of monasticism to supplant or compete with the Patrician foundations of the previous century. Of this 'familia Choluim Chille' Iona was the centre. The saint himself returned at least once and probably more often to supervise his 'familia'. Did he set up Iona† to evangelize (*see* note on that Island) or as a 'desertum' or retreat for meditation and scholarship? It seems that only rarely did he cross Drumalbyn to visit the Picts of the east. Such names in Argyll and the Isles as 'Kilchaluimchille' or variations thereof — seem genuinely to indicate his missionary foundations, but in the east we do not find this but rather names like Inchcolm which are more likely to refer to some Pictish saint called Colm. The picture, then, of Columba as the pioneer missionary converting all over modern Scotland is far from true. Think of him as the Ab, or religious leader, of a powerful group of monasteries most of which were widely scattered through Ireland and as a scholar who maintained the high tradition of scholarship which he had inherited from his childhood education at Maghbile, Clonfert and Glasnevin. There is a poem, the 'Altus Prosator', which may be by him and fragments of the psalms, preserved in the battler known as the Cathach, may also be his — possibly the manuscript which he illicitly copied.

COMGALL. *See* Aileach an Naoimh.

COMYN, Walter, Earl of Menteith. *See* Inchmahome.

CONCHUBAR. *See* Dun Dearduil.

CONSTANTINE (Saint). Sixth century. The Old Parish Church of Govan is dedicated to Saint Constantine and contains a sarcophagus with twelfth century decoration which is reputed to be his. His life, which is quite legendary, makes him king of Cornwall (where place names of Constantine and Mirren are found) and before conversion a very evil ruler. After a dramatic conversion he came to Scotland via Wales and Ireland. Tradition makes him a friend of Kentigern and of Mirren of Paisley†.

COOPER, James. *See* Lee, Robert; Primmer, Jacob.

CORMAC. *See* Aileach an Naoimh.

COUPAR ANGUS ABBEY (Perthshire). Cistercian, founded 1164 by Malcolm IV. A daughter house of Melrose†. Like other Scottish abbeys it suffered at the hands of the English in the Wars of Independence; there seems little evidence for the tradition that it was burned by the Reformers. The present parish church stands on the site, but all that is left of the mediaeval buildings is a fragment of the gatehouse; most of the small town seems to have been built from the pilfered masonry.

CRAIGLUSCAR (Fife). *See* Durie, George.

CRAWFORD, Sir John. *See* Sciennes.

CRIEFF. *See* Angus, John.

CROCKETFORD (Stewartry of Kirkcudbright). *See* Simpson, Elspeth.

CROCKETT, S. R. *See* Balmaghie Church; Shalloch on Minnoch.

CROMARTY. An attractive little town, near oil-development but as yet unspoilt, at the tip of the Black Isle, overlooked by two rocks, the North and South Sutors, which guard the Firth. On these great headlands and in their caves Hugh Miller (1802–56) as a boy began his study of the rocks. Today his statue looks down on the town and his cottage (NTS) is a museum. Miller's sea-captain father was lost with his ship when the boy was only five and he owed much to the wise and firm guidance of two uncles, simple, godly men but by no means unlettered. He refused their offer of college and at 17 became a journeyman mason, getting to know much of north Scotland and something of Midlothian as he travelled from job to job. It was back-breaking work which made him prematurely old and at 32 he made the strange transition from stonemason to bank-clerk. He was already finding a creative outlet in literary work and in detailed, scientific study of geology and in both fields his ability was soon recognized. His third great interest, religion, was fanned to flame by the prospect of disruption in the Church of Scotland. The Evangelical Party, who were soon to become the Free Church, invited him to edit their newspaper *The Witness* and much of his best work appeared in its columns, e.g. the well-known but now dated 'Old Red Sandstone'. In *My Schools and Schoolmasters* (1852) he produced an autobiography which is an important document for social conditions in the early nineteenth century. Miller, who had married in Cromarty, moved to the capital, where he became a well recognized figure in the streets of the New Town. His last, unfinished work, *The Testimony of the Rocks*, revealed the tension between the science and the religion of his day. The new church for which he laboured and which he loved would accept no evidence which might throw doubt on Genesis as a historical and factual account of Creation . . . but there were the fossils in the rocks about which Miller had written so much. In agony of mind, torn between two loyalties, Miller shot himself in his home in Tower Street, Portobello. He was buried in Grange

Hugh Miller of Cromarty, after a photograph by Octavius Hill

Cemetery beside many of his Free Church friends. His contemporaries avoided recognizing his dilemma by assuring everyone he was insane. In Cromarty, the parish church is of interest and the shell of the Gaelic Chapel. Gaelic was not heard here until the time of the Clearances when a local millowner encouraged the displaced to resettle and built the chapel for them.

CROSSRAGUEL ABBEY (Ayrshire). Extensive ruins of Cluniac Abbey, offshoot of Paisley†. Pronounce it 'raygel' for the name commemorates an Irish saint Riaghail, identified, perhaps wrongly, with Rule or Regulus†. Equally incorrect is the tradition that it means 'royal cross'. Founded in 1244 by Duncan, Earl of Carrick, the building suffered greatly at the hands of the English in 1306 when Robert Bruce contested the earldom of Carrick. The church was then rebuilt after a simple rectangular plan. A century later the choir was again rebuilt on a grander scale with an unusual feature, a polygonal east end. Not long before the Reformation the church was divided into two by a cross-wall which still stands, thus providing a more compact chapel for the saying of the monks' office. The number of monks can never have been large — in the fifteenth century it was 10 — and the ruins of 'corrodiars'' houses may indicate an attempt to make fuller use of the buildings as well as an effort to raise extra revenue. Corrodiars were, in essence, paying guests who were provided here (as at Cleeve Abbey in Somerset) with comfortable little private suites of two rooms and toilet. At the Reformation they are mentioned as the 'pur men that hes the yardis'. Maybole is the heart of the Kennedy country, a lowland family as powerful as any highland clan. The last Abbot before the Reformation was William Kennedy, a man of outstanding ability who foretold the coming of 'veray gret trublis'. His nephew, Quintin Kennedy†, was the first Commendator. His successor Allan Stewart was shut up by the Kennedys in Dunure Castle, and roasted on a spit in an effort to make him hand over the Abbey lands; he was basted with oil to keep him from going on fire, and perhaps because of this he survived.

CROSTHWAITE (Cumberland). *See* Kentigern.

CULFARGIE (Perthshire). *See* Moncrieff, Alexander.

CULLODEN (Inverness-shire). *See* Rose, Hugh.

CUMBRAE, Isle of. On the Greater Cumbrae island, near Millport, stands the modern Cathedral of Argyll and the Isles, consecrated in 1876. About the middle of last century the Earl of Glasgow, a devout Episcopalian, built not only his own domestic chapel in the grounds of his estate, The Garrison, but also a tiny cathedral, with collegiate buildings intended for a theological college. Nine years after the consecration the Earl suffered financial disaster which necessitated selling all his Cumbrae estates. Only with difficulty was the building with its immediate grounds saved for the Episcopal Church, and it was quite without support for clergy. Previously, in its heyday, there had been up to eight priests, 20 students and a resident choir. After some years of semidereliction the wealthy bishop Chinnery-Haldane† restored the buildings and paid

for the services of a provost in the person of his friend, Rev. T. I. Ball, who also took charge of St Andrews Episcopal Church in Millport. While the college buildings were popular as a place of retreat they proved too remote for a theological college and this was removed to Glenalmond and then to Coates Hall, Edinburgh.

CURITAN [Kiritinus, Curdy, Bonifacius] *c.* 660–740. Bede, in his *History* tells how King Nechtan macDerile in 710, desiring to convert his Pictish kingdom to Roman usage which had been recommended by the Synod of Whitby, wrote to Abbot Ceolfrid at Wearmouth for guidance on the new customs and for master-builders to build him a church 'after the Roman style' which might be dedicated to St Peter. From other sources it appears that among those sent to the king was a Pict named Curitan or Kiritinus, who himself had accepted the Roman customs and taken the name of Boniface. One account states that Curitan built a church at the mouth of the River Gobriat, i.e. Invergowrie. The ancient ruin at Dargie, now little better than an eyesore, occupies this site. Until recently it possessed a stone with a carving of three figures, the centre one being locally regarded as St Curdy — the pet-name for Curitan. This stone has been removed for safety to the National Museum. He may next have visited King Nechtan at Perth before proceeding back along Strathmore to establish Restenneth†, which may well have been the church 'after the Roman style' which Nechtan had requested. He remained in this district for some time, then moved north to settle in the Black Isle at Rosemarkie, where perhaps he refounded an earlier Celtic settlement of St Moluag. Outside Rosemarkie church stands one of the best examples of the later (Class 2) Pictish slab stones with both pagan and Christian symbols. Dedications to a saint, or churches named after him, must always be viewed with some caution as they are no real proof that the person was actually there, but there are traces of the cult of this saint, and perhaps of his presence at Tobar Churadain (Glen Urquhart), Kilcurdy (Avoch) and Kingoodie (Invergowrie) — this last appears in the seventeenth century as Kill-curdy. There are also early St Peter foundations which may well have been connected with him at Peterculter, Fyvie, Meigle, Tealing etc. As 'Boniface', Curitan is often confused with continental saints of the same name, resulting in such absurd deductions as that he was a Jew who became Pope. The Aberdeen Breviary (1510) gives an incredible and glamorized version of his life. Boece also 'worked up' his biography. He must have been of some importance in the Celtic *v* Roman controversy as he was among the British representatives at the famous Synod of Birr (697) along with King Bruide and Adamnan†.

CUTHBERT. 634–87. A tradition that the saint was born in Ireland is almost certainly erroneous and the probability is that it was near Maelros, or Old Melrose; local tradition claims Wrangholm in Smailholm parish. Cuthbert became a monk at Melrose† under the Ab Eata and later he succeeded Boisil (remembered in St Boswell's) as Prior. Bede wrote a *Life of Cuthbert* and says he checked it from memories of those who had known him. In it he relates stories and miracles of the saint's remarkable journeys through Scotland: 'He often did the rounds of the villages, sometimes on horseback, more often on foot, preaching the way of truth to those who had gone astray . . . He made a point of searching out those steep and rugged places in the hills which other preachers dreaded to visit because of their poverty and squalor . . . Sometimes he would be away a fortnight or a month living with the rough hill folk'. Kirkcudbright and other place names in Galloway connect with Cuthbert, and Bede tells us that he went by boat to 'the land of the Niduari, a tribe of the Picts'. This used to be thought to be the Nith, but as it is now believed that there never were Picts in Galloway the journey is held to be up the east coast, to Fife or Angus — Earlsferry has been suggested as the place. On another occasion he spent some time in Carlisle and he perhaps founded the school which continued until recently as Carlisle Grammar School. Eventually he was placed in charge of the Northumbrian mission centre on Lindisfarne (or Holy Island) where today a small islet is pointed out as his retreat. When

later he was appointed Bishop of Hexham he managed to exchange duties so that he could again work on the island. After the Synod of Whitby (*see* note on Colman) Cuthbert accepted, apparently enthusiastically, the Roman usages, and this caused a deep cleavage between him and many of his monks and friends. He cut himself off by retiring to a remote 'desertum' on the Farne Islands where he passed his last years as a solitary hermit. In this lonely place he died, tended by the monks of Lindisfarne, where at first he was buried. The Danish invasions made this resting place unsafe and the monks began a journey with the coffin and the relics, keeping constantly on the move. In some cases churches named St Cuthbert's may indicate that the body rested there. For over a century it remained at Chester-le-street. Finally, as the result of a vision a bend of the river Wear was accepted as the place where the saint desired to be buried and in 995 it was placed where the great cathedral of Durham would later arise. The coffin — actually three separate layers — was opened in 1104 and again in 1827 when the skeleton was revealed still with the remains of the robes and with a beautiful pectoral cross. The latter is now in Durham cathedral library along with the inner wooden coffin which is remarkably well preserved and which bears incised figures of the evangelists.

CYNDERYN. *See* Kentigern.

DAIRSIE (Fife). *See* Spottiswoode, John.

DALE, David. 1739–1806. From humble beginnings as a herd-laddie on the hills near his birth-place at Stewarton, Dale rose to be joint proprietor with Arkwright of the famous New Lanark spinning mills. Although it is his son-in-law Robert Owen who receives publicity and credit for the social experiments at New Lanark, it was Dale who pioneered these industrial welfare schemes. He became very rich for his day and gave away much of his wealth to charity. He was a devout Christian who left the Relief Church to be one of the founders of the Old Scots Independents (*see* note on Balchrystie). Through the liberality of one Paterson, a candle-maker, Dale and his friends were able to build a chapel in

Greyfriars Wynd, later Shuttle Street, Glasgow, universally known, because of its benefactor, as the Candle Kirk. For 37 years, in spite of his business commitments, Dale acted as one of its pastors, for the denomination did not approve of a single, paid minister. He taught himself Hebrew and Greek and regularly preached from its pulpit.

DALKEITH (Midlothian). *See* Macleod, Norman.

DALL, Robert. 1745–*c*. 1828. Born in Dundee, he was converted by the evangelist Thomas Hanby during his visit to the town in 1763. Encouraged by the Highland Methodist Duncan Wright, he began to preach in 1772. He wrote 'I shaked myself from the world and went out . . . resolving no attachment should hinder me'. He travelled widely, preaching in all the Methodist circuits and spent 22 out of a long ministry of 56 years north of the border. He was responsible for new societies in Moray, Banff and Aberdeenshire, in Kintyre and Campbeltown, and in Dumfries where he was particularly successful. After tramping there 60 miles from Ayr, he wrote 'I got a room to lodge in, went through the town and invited many to hear preaching on the banks of the Nith, a beautiful spot'. Ordered by Conference to continue in Dumfries — 'I brought my family from Glasgow and preached five months outdoors till winter was very cold'. From the citizens and from most of the clergy he found friendliness and encouragement, but for some unknown reason the Relief — a body usually known for its broadmindedness — led active opposition to his preaching. He built a chapel so economically in 1788–9 that he received the special congratulations of John Wesley himself.

DARGIE (Invergowrie). *See* Curitan.

DAVID [Dewi]. *See* Kentigern.

DAVIDSON, Randall. *See* Tait, A. C.

DEACONESS HOSPITAL, EDINBURGH. *See* Baillie, Lady Grisell (2).

DEER (Aberdeenshire). *See* Drostan.

DEFOE, Daniel. *See* Hepburn, John.

DEIRDRE. *See* Dun Dearduil.

DEVORGILLA. *See* Sweetheart Abbey.

DICK, Robert. 1811–66. Born in Tullibody, but spending his adult life as a baker in Thurso, he was friend by correspondence with Hugh Miller of Cromarty† and other scientists. He published only one learned paper himself but had considerable influence as a naturalist and geologist on others. Dick had a sad life, with an unhappy childhood and later both ill-health and business failure. He deserves to be remembered as an example of a good man martyred by the narrow-minded and bigoted church folk of the north of Scotland in the last century. Like his friend Miller he was a devout Christian, finding his Creator's message in the rocks and in all nature. His confined life in the Thurso bakehouse led him to take long walks before and after Sabbath services and this led to a thinly-veiled denunciation of him from the pulpit of the parish church. Dick never re-entered the church and this resulted in a campaign of persecution against him in the small town. The Free Church people had already withdrawn their custom from his bakery because, unlike Miller, he had remained within the parish church at the Disruption: 'I am very well satisfied with the Church of my fathers', he had said. Now the 'auld kirk' people left him too. When a violent storm destroyed a large cargo of his flour he became bankrupt. After Miller shot himself in Edinburgh because his church insisted on the literal account of Creation as in Genesis, Robert Dick was in great agony of mind. 'Of one thing you may be sure,' he wrote to his sister on hearing of his friend's death, 'the earth as we know it was not made in six ordinary days. The earth is making yet.' He was not satisfied that Darwin had the right answer but he was satisfied that he could keep his faith and still deny the literal truth of Genesis as history. After he had died in poverty the Caithness people began to appreciate how widely this quiet and lonely citizen had been esteemed far beyond their boundaries, and also how badly they themselves had behaved. The parish minister, who visited Dick before he died, made some small restitution when he described him as 'The most humble believer I have ever met'. The biography of Hugh Miller contains no mention of Dick's name and the suggested reason has been that it was composed by a

Free Church supporter unwilling to admit that Miller had any dealings with one from the rival church.

DODDRIDGE, Philip. *See* Gillespie, Thomas.

DOLLAR. *See* Foret, Thomas; Mylne, Andrew.

DONALDSON, James. *See* Barclay, John.

DONEVALDUS. *See* Abernethy.

DOW, Antony. *See* Barclay, John.

DOWDEN, John. 1840–1910. Born Cork, educated Trinity College, curate at St John's, Sligo and — his final appointment in his home country — chaplain to the Lord Lieutenant. He was one of the not inconsiderable number of Church of Ireland clergy who felt frustrated by its obvious Protestantism and transferred to Scotland. It is understandable that it was Bishop Forbes† of Brechin who welcomed him with the post of Pantonian Professor of Theology at Glenalmond. If Dowden be approached through his *Celtic Church in Scotland* or other serious writings he will be recognized for the considerable historical and liturgical scholar which he was, whereas if the approach be through his long controversies in the correspondence columns of *The Scotsman* over the signature 'J. Edenburgen' which annoyed citizens of the capital so intensely, it is difficult to detect any note of Christian charity toward or any understanding of, that branch of the Church which the majority of Scots people had chosen as their own. He had been consecrated Bishop of Edinburgh in 1886, a position which he combined with a lectureship at the Theological College. He concerned himself particularly with the revision of the Scottish Liturgy which was then taking place.

DROSTAN [Trustram, Trust]. Sixth century? Scholars disagree as to whether there ever was such a saint, and if so, where and when we would find him. Is he a

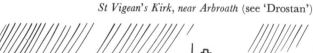

St Vigean's Kirk, near Arbroath (see 'Drostan')

variant of the knight Sir Tristram, so important in the Arthurian legends? This might be possible if we were to place the Round Table in Scotland and give the stories a northern locus; but this few authorities today would accept. (*See* note on Arthur). Or is Drostan the nephew of Columba, who landed from Iona at Aberdour in Buchan and founded the monastery of Deer? *The Book of Deer*, which makes this claim was probably a clever forgery prepared to make just such doubtful historical statements in support of its antiquity. Again, could he be (as G. F. Knight in his *Early Christianising of Scotland* believes) a Pictish saint, earlier than Columba, who came north from Candida Casa to evangelize in Angus and the Mearns? In Kirkcudbrightshire there is a 'Trusty's Hill' with an isolated Pictish stone beside it, well outside the area where such symbol stones are found. Oengus the Culdee, in his *Felire*, writes of 'Trursus and his Three' who are believed to be the saints Colm, Medan and Fergus — all names associated with the north-east. The name appears on the famous stone in the museum of Pictish slabs at St Vigean's (AM) on a small panel at the side. The lettering seems to read

DROSTEN IPE VORET ETT FORCVS.

Of this there are as many interpretations as there are letters in the inscription, ranging from the simple 'Drosten, Ipevoret and Forcus' of Professor Macallister, to 'O Cross, time may destroy thee too' from an editor of the Aberdeen *Journal*. J. Y. Simpson, of chloroform fame, a keen amateur archaeologist, was among those who tried to decipher it. Professor Charles Thomas, a modern authority, doubts if it means anything, and there is increasing suspicion that the lettering was no part of the original monument.

DRUMMOND CASTLE (Perthshire). *See* Stobhall.

DRUMMOND, Henry (1). 1851–95. It is unusual for one who failed his M.A. and left university without a degree to become a professor, and for one who completed, but at some length, his divinity course but never sought ordination not only to influence a large group of ministers in his own day but leave an impression on the Scottish ministry which tends to increase rather

than diminish. Unusual also that this man could be a leading figure in a revival movement and yet never himself confess to a 'conversion experience'. Born in Stirling of the well-known seedsmen family — his brother founded the Drummond Tract Society — Henry Drummond was educated at Stirling High School, Morison's Academy and Edinburgh University; but he could not pass the Humanity examination necessary for the degree. He then studied at New College but did not seek licence as a preacher. The evangelical faith inherited from his forebears was strengthened by his introduction to, and later friendship with, the American evangelist Dwight Moodie. He took part in the 'enquiry room' at the Glasgow campaign of 1873 and accompanied the mission through Scotland and England. His biographer, Professor J. Y. Simpson (whose life pattern was to follow closely that of Drummond) writes 'Sudden conversion he did not doubt, for he saw too many instances but he did not understand it fully since he never personally experienced it'. At this point Drummond intended to be an evangelist, and he had a great power of attracting men — both working men (for whom he held for many years a series of meetings in the old Gaiety Theatre in Chambers' Street, Edinburgh) and students (for whom and with whom he worked in various Students' Movements and settlements). Although he was never a great scientist or a deep thinker he had the ability to 'popularize' the scientific discoveries of his day, and to his own satisfaction to reconcile evolutionary theories with religion. His most influential work *Natural Law in the Spiritual World* would scarcely be accepted as convincing today but it became a best-seller and brought him fame. He was licensed by the Free Church as a preacher but never sought ordination. In spite of this his Church created for him a lectureship in Natural Science at Trinity College, Glasgow, and later erected it into a chair, a post which Drummond occupied, without giving up his voluntary missionary work, until his early death. His greatness lay not in his scholarship, of which he possessed not a great deal either in science or theology, but in understanding men, and in profound and obvious faith in an age when

D

The ruins of Dryburgh Abbey

a narrow and dogmatic Presbyterianism was alienating the younger generation. He left behind him a group of young ministers who were evangelical but tolerant and broad-minded, liberal or, in later years, often socialist in politics, zealous in S.C.M., Y.M.C.A., B.B. and overseas missions — men who in an age of formality dressed often as laymen and who were unashamedly happier among laymen than among their stiffer ecclesiastical brothers. Among those influenced by Drummond were members of the families of Barbours of Bonskeid and the Simpsons, John Kelman, Herbert Gray etc. After three generations it is still possible to recognize ministers of the distinctive Drummond 'stamp'.

DRUMMOND, Henry (2) of Albury. *See* Irving, Edward.

DRYBURGH ABBEY (Berwickshire; AM). Tradition asserts that St Modan, one of Columba's followers evangelized from this centre as long ago as 622, but the first historical mention we have of Dryburgh is its foundation as a house of Premonstraten-

sian Canons from Alnwick around 1150–2. It became the most important Abbey of this order in Scotland although the primacy was always claimed by the lesser Soulseat†. The house consisted of 'canons' not 'monks' i.e. they could act as parish priests and were not enclosed. They were, however, 'canons regular', i.e. they had taken vows of obedience to the rules of their order. They were popularly known as White Canons, or Norbertines, as their founder was St Norbert of Premontré. Dryburgh has little that is interesting or exciting in its history, no outstanding churchman, even (writes Dr Margarite Wood) 'no great piety . . . accumulating lands and quarrelling over them with an intensity worthy of a better cause'. On more than one occasion it was ravaged and burned by the English, but in the end, rather like its neighbour house of Melrose, it died almost of its own volition. The goodwill and bounty of wealthy laymen turned away from the abbeys, whose monks they suspected of idleness, or worse, and for a time benefactions passed to the more popular orders of

Friars. The process of decay was hastened from within by the practice of 'commendation', whereby the resources were diverted to some royal or noble layman while the actual community was run on a shoestring. Finally, monastic lands came to be regarded simply as a hereditary 'perk'. Often it needed no storming reformers to complete the destruction. What they did, in most cases, was to knock out the glass and burn the wooden screens and statues, thereby tragically depriving us of objects of great artistic value. Today Dryburgh is visited as the burial place of Sir Walter Scott and Sir Douglas Haig. *See also* note on Baillie, Lady Grisell (2).

DUMBARTON. *See* Patrick.

DUMFRIES. *See* Dall, Robert; Hepburn, John.

DUN (Angus). *See* Burns, William C.

DUNADD (Argyll). *See* Columba.

DUNBAR, Alexander. *See* Pluscarden Priory.

DUNBLANE. *See* Blane; Leighton, Robert.

DUNCAN, Earl of Carrick. *See* Crossraguel.

DUNCAN, Henry. 1774–1846. Minister for 45 years at Ruthwell† (pronounced Rivvel) Dumfriesshire where the first Scottish savings bank was founded by him in 1810. Dr J. L. Dinwiddie's history of the parish states that there had been banks for savings before his time both in England and on the Continent, but the bank set up in the cottage which served as the parish hall for Ruthwell, was the first to be started on business principles as a viable financial project and so he is legitimately remembered as the founder of the savings bank movement. In his early manhood he had himself been engaged in banking in Liverpool. He was also instrumental in restoring the great Anglo-Saxon Cross of Ruthwell, although his zeal for Freemasonry caused him to have the transom carved with symbols which are obviously inappropriate. He was author of some verse and of 'The Curling Song' which was sung recently when the original cottage was opened (October 1974) as a Henry Duncan Museum by his great-great-great grand-son. There is an obelisk with medallion to him on B724 near Mouswald, a statue outside Dumfries Savings Bank building and a tablet within Ruthwell Church. In his rectorial address at St Andrews University Rudyard Kipling singled out two alumni for special mention — Duncan and Chalmers — in that order.

DUNDAS STREET CONGREGATIONAL CHURCH, GLASGOW. *See* Morison, James.

DUN DEARDUIL (Inverness-shire). At the foot of the pass of Farigaig, above the 'corkscrew' which leaves the older and inland Wade road to descend steeply to Loch Ness, stands the massive rock of Dun Dearduil, topped by the remains of a vitrified fort and more awesome and impressive than its height in feet would justify. Connected with the legendary Celtic heroine Deirdre who fled from her suitor Conchubar, King of Ulster, with the three sons of Uisneach, one of whom, Naoise, was her lover. Through the treachery of Conchubar the brothers were enticed back to Ulster and foully slain. Deirdre composed the famous Gaelic lament when by 'second sight' she warned them of their danger. Both Scotland and Ireland have many places claiming a part in the adventures of Deirdre and Naoise (from whom Loch Ness takes its name), and there is another hill, similarly topped by a vitrified fort and also named after the Celtic heroine-goddess, some miles south, up Glen Nevis. The oldest version of the many variations of this folk-tale is in the twelfth century *Book of Leinster*.

DUNDRENNAN ABBEY (Stewartry of Kirkcudbright). *See* Sweetheart Abbey.

DUNFALLANDY (Perthshire). *See* Restalrig.

DUNFERMLINE. *See* deBothwell, Robert; Durie, George; Erskine, Ralph; Gillespie Church; deKeldeleth, Robert; Margaret; Primmer, Jacob.

DUNKELD CATHEDRAL (Perthshire; AM). Mediaeval cathedral on ancient Pictish site. A list of Pictish kings ascribes its foundation to Constantine who ascended the throne in 789. It was refounded with a bishop by Kenneth Macalpine.

After the Danish invasions had made Iona unsafe as a centre the authority of the church passed to Dunkeld. One tradition states that Columba's relics were brought there. In the period of Roman ascendency Dunkeld, like Abernethy† was subordinated to St Andrews†. The choir, now used as the parish church, dates from the thirteenth century, and the nave, now ruined, from the fifteenth century. Like Elgin, it was a 'secular' cathedral; that is, it was not under the control of any order of 'regular' or cloistered clergy, but had its own constitution with secular priests under a dean. Its most notable bishop was Gavin Douglas. The edict for the despoiling of the buildings at the Reformation is still extant: 'we pray yow tak doun the haill images and bring furth to the kirk-zayrd and burn thaym oppinly. And siclyk cast doun the altaris and purge the kyrk of all kynd of monuments of idolatyre . . . but ze tak guid heyd that neither the dasks, windocks, nor durris, be anyways hurt or broken, either glassin wark or iron wark.' This clearly shows the Reformers' policy: to destroy only those features which were in their opinion connected with erroneous doctrine. The loss, however, at Dunkeld was great for it must have included Bishop Lauder's great reredos showing the 24 miracles of St Columba surrounded by carved angelic figures.

DUNNICHEN (Angus). *See* Restenneth.

DUNNING (Perthshire). *See* Serf.

DUNNOTTAR (Kincardine). *See* Barclay, Robert.

DUNPELDER (East Lothian). *See* Thenew.

DUNS SCOTUS, John. Thirteenth century. Franciscan theologian, not to be confused with the Irish Scotus Erigena of the ninth century. Little is known of his life except his birthplace, Maxton, near Roxburgh, and that he studied at Paris and Oxford. He differs from the classic theology of Thomas Aquinas in his emphasis on love and the will rather than on reason and knowledge. He defended the doctrine of the Immaculate Conception against Bernard and the Cistercians who argued against it.

DUNURE CASTLE (Ayrshire). *See* Crossraguel Abbey.

DURIE, George. *fl.* 1550. Nephew of Archbishop James Beaton (1)†, archdeacon of St Andrews, abbot of Dunfermline 1526–60, the last regular holder of that office. He owned the estate of Craigluscar in Carnock parish, and it was rumoured that he hid there the relics of St Margaret† until they could be smuggled to France. There also lived his unofficial wife and

Dunkeld Cathedral

family. After 1560 he was put in ward possibly under the surveillance of his Protestant kinsman, David Durie. His son, John Durie, inherited his father's zeal for the old faith, and after education at Paris and Louvain, returned to Britain as a Jesuit missionary. He was charged to leave the country on pain of death. A 'Jesuit Durie' is recorded as being involved in an attempt to release Queen Mary of Scots.

DURIE, John. d. 1600. Born Mauchline, educated Ayr, he became a monk of Dunfermline during the abbacy of George Durie†, said by Spottiswoode to be his cousin (from whose son, John, he must be distinguished). He was suspected of leanings toward 'the new teaching' and was imprisoned. At the Reformation he was released and in 1563 we find him in Edinburgh accused of an attack on two men 'vpon the hie streit quhair thai were gayand to thair beddis'. The account of the strange incident is confused, but it appears to have been a skirmish between the Queen's party and their opponents. In 1567 he is 'exhorter' at Penicuik, two years later, minister at Colinton, then at Leith and in 1573 one of the ministers of St Giles. His forthright sermons were displeasing to James VI and as the result of a particularly outspoken one in 1579 he was summoned to bring a copy to the royal presence. In the end he only handed this to the king under threat of imprisonment. He was again summoned before the Privy Council and banished from the city. When the political wind changed and he was allowed to return his entry was something of a triumph as he was escorted back from the Netherbow to St Giles by a crowd singing Psalm 124. In 1583 he was again exiled from Edinburgh and, joining his son-in-law James Melville† in St Andrews, he continued on to Montrose where he remained until his death. His three sons all became ministers and his two daughters both married ministers: Elizabeth's husband, James Melville, wrote of his father-in-law 'The mair I think on him the mair I thank God that ever I knew him'.

DYSART (Fife). *See* Serf.

EALDFRITH [Flann Fina macOssa]. *See* Adamnan.

EARLSFERRY (Fife). *See* Cuthbert.

EATA. *See* Cuthbert; Melrose.

EBBA [Aebbe]. *See* Coldingham.

ECHOBANK CEMETERY, EDINBURGH. *See* Cairns, John.

EDWIN. *See* Aidan.

EGGLESPETHER (Angus). *See* Restenneth.

EITHNE. *See* Aileach an Naoimh.

ELPHINSTONE, William. 1431–1514. For a short period Bishop of Ross, then from 1483 of Aberdeen. His biography was written by Hector Boece whom he had appointed first Principal of the new university he had founded at Aberdeen. Elphinstone was the illegitimate son of a canon of Glasgow Cathedral. The fact that his parents are mentioned without embarrassment indicates that by the middle of the fifteenth century clerical celibacy was accepted in Scotland as nominal and the future bishop seems to have enjoyed a normal and happy home life in Glasgow. When the university in that town was founded in 1451 he was among the first enrolled students. After graduating in Arts he was ordained and returned to college to study canon law. In 1463 he left for France to continue his studies and on his return he was appointed Official of the diocese, an important office which carried with it a seat in Parliament. Other important legal

King's College, Old Aberdeen

and clerical appointments fell to this brilliant and scholarly priest; he was made Privy Councillor, Bishop of Ross, then of Aberdeen, and became friend and adviser to James III and later to James IV. His influence on the political life of Scotland was great, but in his diocese he was remembered as 'the good bishop', founding Aberdeen University and equipping it with a glorious chapel and the scholastic buildings of King's College, reroofing and restoring the nearby cathedral, reforming the Chapter and improving the musical services. He built a bridge over the Dee and introduced the printing press to Scotland. When over 80 he exerted himself on behalf of the moderate party to avert the hot temper which led to the disaster of Flodden, for which he was dubbed an unpatriotic dotard. His tomb, despoiled at the Reformation, has been restored during the present century.

ENOCH. See Thenew.

ERROL (Perthshire). See Caird, John.

ERSKINE [Areskine], **Ebenezer.** 1680–1754. One of the four Original Seceders from the Church of Scotland and brother of Ralph†, minister of Dunfermline. Their father, Henry, was minister just over the Border at Cornhill and suffered greatly through the Act of Uniformity, being held for a time on the Bass Rock and tortured with the thumbikins. He was deeply evangelical and was the means of the conversion of Thomas Boston (see note on Ettrick). After nine years of study at Edinburgh, Ebenezer became chaplain to the influential Rothes family. He was called to Portmoak, the historic parish by the side of Loch Leven which had been connected with the labours of St Serf†, and ordained in 1703. A 'conversion experience' occurred a few years later, the result, he said, of his overhearing a conversation on godly matters between his brother Ralph and his wife: 'I choose Christ as my prophet for instruction, illumination and direction, I embrace him as my great High Priest to be washed and justified by his blood and righteousness. I embrace him as my King to rule and reign within me. I take a whole Christ with all his laws and all

his crosses and afflictions.' From this time his ministry was exercised with great power and love which drew large crowds to Portmoak to hear him and share in his Sacrament sessions. Before he left for Stirling in 1731 the controversies which were to culminate in the Secession had diminished some of his popularity. Theologically he was now classed as a 'Marrow Man', a follower of Thomas Boston's 'gospel of free grace'. Emphasizing the contrast between the legalism of the Jew and the free gift of grace upon which the Christian depended, the Marrow Men appeared to their opponents to despise all good works. Auchterarder Presbytery, where they were in the majority, compelled its ministers to sign a formula that 'I believe it is not sound or orthodox to teach that we must forsake sin in order to come to Christ'. When the General Assembly refused to sanction this Erskine, Moncrieff†, Wilson of Perth and Fisher of Kinclaven met in December 1733 at Gairneybridge† to plan secession. He and his friends were also suspect because they objected strongly to the revival of patronage in the Church under an Act which followed the Union of the Parliaments. To them the State Church was now not only in error theologically but held in thrall to the State. The General Assembly of 1734 deposed the seceding ministers — who insisted that they were still part of the Church of Scotland but in rightful defiance of the Church courts — but in the following year through the influence of Willison of Dundee† the ban was lifted. The Seceders, by this time, were rapidly organizing themselves into a separate denomination and refused to rejoin their parent body. They were, however, reluctant to give up their manses, churches and parish connections. Ebenezer Erskine preached in his Stirling Church until 1740 when he found the doors locked against him and thereafter officiated from a meeting-house. Like the other Seceders he opposed the '45 Rising and even offered to raise a regiment for the Duke of Cumberland whom he much admired. The offer was refused. In the controversy over the Burgess Oath he took the opposite side from Moncrieff, allowing freedom of conscience on the matter and so leading the Burghers against the Anti-Burghers.

ERSKINE, Henry. *See* Erskine, Ebenezer.

ERSKINE [Areskine], **Ralph.** 1685–1752. Younger brother of Ebenezer†. He entered Edinburgh University at 15, already of a religious disposition. In his boyhood notebook he wrote, 'Lord, put Thy fear in my heart. Let my thoughts be holy and let me do for Thy glory all that I do. Give a good judgement and memory, a firm belief in Jesus Christ and an assured token of Thy love.' After the ordination of Ebenezer to Portmoak, Ralph spent two

long vacations in the manse at the foot of the Lomond Hills. In 1711, at the age of 27, he accepted a call to the second charge at Dunfermline. The documents were in the name of Mr Areskine, the old form which he later dropped. Double charges were common in larger burghs in former days. The ministers alternated in conducting worship but shared one church; each had his own flock. It was not an easy time at first in Dunfermline as there had been controversy between the previous ministers over Presbytery versus Episcopacy, and the first charge had just been filled the previous year by the Rev. Thomas Buchanan. On his death in 1714 Ralph was chosen for his successor and had as colleague the Rev. James Wardlaw, who, while differing theologically, proved a helpful friend. The two drew up a document to avoid trouble between them: 'Rules and Principles

agreed upon betwixt Mr J W and Mr R E in order to the maintaining of a good understanding betwixt them . . . That they shall not receive any ill report of one another — no, not from the wife of our bosom or dearest friend . . . That we shall not be under the management of our wife's or any other's advice . . .' Ralph had a large parish and treated the pastoral ministry very seriously. There are notes of his visiting the prison, the outlying districts and the young: 'this minister of Christ did not overlook the lambs of his flock'. His catechetical questions to the young seem strange today —

Q: 'Are you so young that you may not be sick and die?'

Q: 'Are young folk exempted from death and the grave?'

Q: 'Have you not seen infants laid in the cold dust?'

Q: 'Are you so young that you may not go to Hell?'

We must remember that children lived much closer to the sight of death in Erskine's day and in spite of the awesomeness of such questions, Ralph was the least forbidding of the Seceders. There are anecdotes told of his love of music and the difficulties it sometimes occasioned. It was in answer to an invitation from him that Whitefield† came north, and later he deplored his brethren's attitude to him. He was a good Latin scholar and a writer of spiritual songs, if not of a high quality:

'Sweet was the hour I freedom felt,
    To call my Jesus mine,
To see his smiling face and melt
    In pleasures all divine.'

Although not among the 'four originals' Ralph soon joined the Secession. In Dunfermline he continued to preach in the Abbey while also holding services later in the day in the new meeting-house (replaced later by the Erskine Church). When Wardlaw would not leave the National Church or advise his elders to do so, Ralph for the first time failed in Christian understanding and used the pulpit they shared to denounce him. He died before his elder brother, who exclaimed when it was told to him, 'And is Ralph gone? . . . He was first in Christ and now he is first in Glory.'

ERSKINE, Thomas. 1788–1870. Laird of Linlathen, a mile inland from Monifieth. An active, evangelical layman who exercised considerable influence on Scottish thought of his times. A lifelong bachelor, an advocate who never practised, he was author, among other works, of *Internal Evidence of Revealed Religion* (1820) and *The Gift of the Holy Spirit* (1830). No branch of the Scottish Church secured his complete loyalty. He began as a member of the Independent Ward Chapel, Dundee, which he was asked to leave because of his broad theological views; he then worshipped for a time at St Mary's Episcopal Church, Broughty Ferry, and finally he attached himself to the Established Church. He had friends in all camps and was on intimate terms with many of the great literary and ecclesiastical figures of his day. He was interested in education and founded several schools in Angus. He was a profound admirer of McLeod Campbell† whose defence before the General Assembly he financed and for whose retirement he built Achnashie in Rosneath†. His beautiful Linlathen estate has long supplied Dundee with water from its reservoirs, and his home, now a derelict shell, keeps its memories of Thomas Carlyle, Dean Ramsay†, George Gilfillan† and many others who were entertained under its roof.

ERTHA. *See* Blane.

ETTRICK KIRK (Selkirkshire). The most peaceful of country churchyards encircling a seemly church with no interior fol-de-rols. With it will ever be connected the memory of Thomas Boston, the 'Marrow Man'. Born in 1676 he came here, to the predecessor of the present building, in 1707, and remained in this upland backwater until he preached his last sermon from the manse window in April 1732, to be laid a month later in the plot which bears his name. In his previous parish of Simprin he had chanced on a copy of *The Marrow of Modern Divinity* by Edward Fisher of Oxford, and this had greatly influenced his thought on the lines of 'free grace' (*see* note on Ebenezer Erskine). Although Boston died a year before the Secession, he was its inspiration. He drew great crowds to this remote place for his communion seasons — a thousand

Thomas Boston of Ettrick

on one occasion — but he was never called to any more influential sphere. The valley is now much depopulated, the charge linked and the manse let. Here also lie Hogg the Shepherd, and Tibbie Shiel and Will O'Whaup.

EWAN [Owein] son of Urien. *See* Thenew.

EWING, Greville. 1767–1841. 'He organized a strong Congregational Church out of its beginnings in an evangelical mission, giving it power, and purpose and permanence' writes Nelson Gray, Ewing's biographer, of this minister who has been called the 'Father of Scottish Congregationalism'. Ewing was born in the High Street of Edinburgh and brought up by a step-mother who used to take the boy to Heriot's grounds to hear George Whitefield's† open-air services. As a result of this evangelical influence she left her family church of Greyfriars and joined Lady Glenorchy's Chapel†, which, while part of the Established Church, opened its pulpit to all denominations. Completing his craftsman apprenticeship as a seal-maker Greville Ewing studied for the ministry, meanwhile assisting in the evangelical work of the Chapel and helping Lady Darcy Maxwell, Lady Glenorchy's friend, in her work among the poor. Many years later Ewing was to take Lady Maxwell's daughter as his third wife. The young minister, therefore, was early drawn into this vigorous evangelical society which was strangely different from the Church of which it was technically a part. When he was invited to become assistant to the Rev. Thomas Jones, minister at the Chapel, his models were not so much his Presbyterian brethren as the visiting English evangelists of various denominations. Soon he was regarded as colleague in the Chapel and therefore avoided having to seek a 'patron' to 'present' him to a parish. He was already tending to resent Patronage and incline to independency. In 1794 his friend William Innes of Stirling, whose sister became his first wife, introduced him to Robert Haldane† and Ewing became one of the circle of young men whom the Haldanes gathered round them. He was involved in Haldane's scheme for mission in Bengal and when this was stopped by the government he was chosen as tutor in the seminary for training lay preachers which met at first in his house in Rose Court, Edinburgh and which later followed him to Glasgow. In 1798 Ewing had severed his connection with the Church of Scotland and accepted Haldane's offer to take charge of the Glasgow Tabernacle, erected on the site of a riding academy at the corner of Ann Street and Jamaica Street. It was not long, however, before disagreement broke out between Ewing and Robert Haldane who had supplied the money for the seminary, the Tabernacles and other schemes. Ewing resented any hint of Patronage, while Haldane on his part must have felt that little effort was being made to make the Glasgow Tabernacle self-supporting. In addition, both Haldanes were turning to adult 'believers' baptism' with which Ewing disagreed and there were differences in their views on church government. Haldane tended to the position of John Glas† with a 'plurality of preaching elders' in every church (the 'Scotch Baptist' position), while Ewing held to one minister supported by a number of deacons. Although Ewing had ceased to use the title 'Reverend' after leaving the Church of Scotland, he believed in a settled ministry rather than a series of visiting preachers. He accepted the degree of D.D. from an American University. In 1809 he resigned

from the Tabernacle and those who followed him built a new hall in Nile Street. He died without accepting the offer of reconciliation which Haldane made to him.

EXMOUTH. *See* Maxwell, Willielma.

FEARN (Ross-shire). *See* Hamilton, Patrick.

FERADACH. *See* Aberlemno.

FERGUSON, David. *See* Angus, John.

FERRIER, Robert. *See* Balchrystie.

FETTERCAIRN (Kincardine). *See* Barclay, John.

FISHER, James. *See* Erskine, Ebenezer.

FORBES, Alexander Penrose. 1817–75. Bishop of Brechin in the Scottish Episcopal Church. Son of a Scottish Judge, born Edinburgh, educated at the Academy there and at Glasgow University. Intended for service with the East India Company, but when ill health caused his return he read for Holy Orders at Oxford. After a brief curacy in Oxford in 1846 he returned to Scotland as rector of the Episcopal church at Stonehaven, but within a year we find him again in England at the Anglo-Catholic church of St Saviour's, Leeds. This was also a brief ministry, for in 1847, through the recommendation of Mr Gladstone, he was elected Bishop of Brechin, the

Bishop Forbes of Brechin

diocese whose centre was the growing industrial city of Dundee where his life-work was to lie. The central congregation of Episcopalians in the town then met above a bank in the High Street but through the vision and the labours of Forbes the new church of St Paul's was completed in 1855 and consecrated as the cathedral ten years later. He became very much the father-figure of episcopacy not only in Dundee but over a much wider area. Forbes had been much influenced by the 'Oxford' or 'Tractarian' movement which had divided the Anglican Church into those who stressed the Protestant link, favoured simplicity of ritual and traditional Reformed theology and the Anglo-catholics or Tractarians who considered themselves rather Catholic than Protestant, sought to recover a fullness of ritual which, they asserted, was in the early Church and developed a theology akin to that then favoured by Rome. One of Forbes' Oxford friends was John Keble, a leader of the movement and Forbes led his diocese and the Scottish Episcopal Church to accept the new ways. He did not achieve this without considerable bitterness and opposition. In 1857 he used phrases in the charge to his clergy which the other bishops interpreted as 'transubstantiation' or the doctrine of Rome on the Real Presence of Christ in the Sacrament. Led by Bishop Wordsworth† they argued that 'we have no authority whereby we can require it to be believed that the substance of Christ's Body and Blood, still less His entire Person as God and Man, is made to exist with, in or under the material substances of Bread and Wine'. The Bishops feared that their church might be brought to the point of adoration of the elements as was the Roman practice. The controversy was bitter but eventually in most points it was Forbes' views which prevailed. Again in the face of opposition he introduced into Dundee the first Protestant nuns, a sister-hood of nine with a Mother Superior to help with the social work of the city.

FORBES, Patrick. 1564–1635. Laird of Corse, Aberdeenshire (where the name Forbes is always pronounced as two syllables) and elder brother of 'Willie the Merchant' who built Craigievar Castle.

Andrew Melville† was his second cousin. After Stirling Grammar School Forbes studied under Melville at Glasgow University and followed him to St Andrews. When the Melvilles fled to England he went with them and continued his studies at Oxford. On his return, in obedience to his father's wish he gave up study, settled down at Montrose and married. In 1598 he in-herited and returned to Aberdeenshire where he was called in as a prominent and educated layman to help the Reformed Church which was short of ministers and, in that area, struggling against a revival of Romanism. In 1611 he agreed to ordina-tion and was presented to Keith, where he wrote a commentary to the Apocalypse in addition to several anti-Catholic pamph-lets. He was accepted by the 'Reforming party' because of his kinship to Melville but he was also regarded as safe by King James, who appointed him to the See of Aberdeen in 1618. He was a moderate man for his times, strangely inconsistent in some ways. He supported the burning of witches, disagreed with the toleration of non-conformists, searched out and punished papish conventicles and Jesuit priests. Yet his views on bishops were by no means those of Laud and the Anglicans: he held that Apostolic Succession was only of those 'whose obedience and life are those of the apostles'. On the nature of the true church his views were like those of Calvin. While convinced of the right of the king to rule in certain matters — and he spoke in the General Assembly in favour of James' hated Five Articles of Perth — he had courage to give judgement against what the king had directed in a certain case, saying that he owed his appointment to the king but his conscience to God. He was among the best of the early post-reforma-tion bishops and had his type continued over the next generations much division and bloodshed might have been avoided.

FORDOUN (Kincardine). *See* Logie Airth.

FORET [Forrest], **Thomas.** d. 1538/1539. Augustinian canon of Inchcolm and vicar of Dollar, a parish served from the island monastery. The family estate of Foret in the Parish of Logie was not far from Falkland Palace and his father had held office under James IV. Foret studied at Cologne and it was when he returned and entered the Inchcolm monastery that his orthodoxy began to be questioned. It was said that he was infested by heresy through reading Augustine and the Scriptures in the abbey library. His name is remembered in Dollar district in 'Vicar's Bridge', a delightful stone bridge across the

River Devon which he is said to have built to allow him to travel more directly to and from the abbey. The bridge remained quite solid until recently when the County Council rather cruelly demolished it for a modern structure which could quite easily have been constructed slightly down the river without harming Foret's bridge. Foret was in touch with the canons of the nearby Abbey of Cambuskenneth who were suspect of heresy, and with Thomas Cocklaw, priest of Tullibody, who was also accused of false doctrine. Foret figures in Foxe's *Book of Martyrs* and it was at his examination that the Bishop of Dunkeld was credited with the almost unbelievable words 'I thank God that I never knew what the Old and New Testament was'. Foret was given several warnings, by his own abbot and by more formal episcopal admonitions. He was accused of declining to take offerings, of teaching the scriptures and parts of the service to his people in the English tongue. He was executed on the

Castlehill, Edinburgh, after trial before Cardinal Beaton, the Lord Chancellor and the Bishops of Glasgow and Dunblane.

FORT WILLIAM. *See* MacLeod, John.

FOULIS EASTER CHURCH (Angus). West of the ancient parish of Liff, with which it is now united, stands the church of Foulis Easter with the jougs still chained to the wall and an early 'preaching cross' in the graveyard. The dedication to St Marnon or Marnock means little but there is evidence of a church here at least from the twelfth century. The present building dates from the time the charge became collegiate, *c.* 1450; it had a provost and seven prebendaries. It still possesses several items of interest and importance: an aumbry in the north wall, considered to be the best in Scotland, a set of saints and apostles painted on wood, a defaced wooden panel of the Trinity *c.* 1540 in which the Virgin is suckling the child, and best of all an immense crucifixion on oaken boards which once formed the rood screen. Of date about 1480 it is considered one of the best of such late-mediaeval paintings and has recently been successfully restored. It probably escaped at the Reformation through the influence of the local laird, Lord Gray, who was *persona grata* to the reformers. *Drawing of church, overleaf.*

FOSSOWAY. *See* Serf.

FRASER, Simon, Lord Lovat. *See* Macdonald, Hugh.

FRASERBURGH. *See* Jolly, Alexander.

FREEMINION (Dumfriesshire). *See* Renwick, James.

FREE NORTH CHURCH, INVERNESS. *See* MacLeod, John.

FREE ST JOHN'S CHURCH, EDINBURGH. *See* Guthrie, Thomas.

FYVIE (Aberdeenshire). *See* Curitan.

GAIRNEYBRIDGE (Kinross-shire). South of Kinross on the A9, but hidden from the motorway M9, stands a high obelisk on the site of the cottage where, in December 1733, Ebenezer Erskine† with Moncrieff†, Fisher and Wilson finally resolved to 'secede' from the Church of Scotland and to form an 'Associate Presbytery'.

Later in the same century the school in the little hamlet had two notable masters — John Brown, later of Haddington† and Michael Bruce†.

GARDNER, Jean and **Katie.** *See* Innes, Andrew.

GEDDES, John. d. 1799. Of all the Catholic bishops in the days before emancipation, John Geddes, titular Bishop of Morocco, coadjutor to Bishop Hay† in the Scottish Lowland District, was the one most able and willing to mix and fit in with the cultured Protestant way of life in eighteenth century Edinburgh. He was recalled to Scotland after a period as Rector of the Scots College at Valladolid which he had re-established. For many years Bishop Hay centred himself on Aberdeen, leaving Geddes to Modern Athens in its Golden Age, but worrying, it is said, not a little about his 'worldliness'. In spite of his Catholic faith he was a welcome guest at the supper parties of such personalities as Lord Monboddo, where in 1786 he met Robert Burns and friendship sprang up between the strangely different men. The Bishop wrote of Burns as 'a very good poet . . . he has made many excellent poems in old Scotch. I shall send them to you.' In one of his many letters to Mrs Dunlop, Burns wrote 'I have outraged that gloomy, fiery Protestantism enough already . . . I don't tell her that the first [i.e. finest] cleric I ever saw was a Popish Bishop, Geddes.' Clarinda (Mrs Maclehose) wrote to Burns 'When you see Bishop Geddes ask him if he remembers a lady at Mrs Kemp's on a Sunday night who listened to every word he uttered . . . [he] returned that glance of cordial warmth which assured me he was pleased with my delicate flattery.' One can understand why his older colleague was worried! In 1789 Burns himself borrowed the Bishop's copy of the Edinburgh edition of his poems and sent it back with a long letter and some additional verses. Abbé Macpherson wrote of Geddes

Foulis Easter Church

Bishop John Geddes

'His learning was great, his piety, affability, humility . . . were all qualities so engaging that it appeared impossible for anyone who had an opportunity of being in his company not to respect and love him.' Bishop Geddes was as liberal as Bishop Hay was conservative. He would have introduced music which was then almost unknown in Scottish Catholic services, but it was disallowed, and desired liturgical changes were also vetoed by his superior who outlived him by 12 years. All his life he had been fond of walking and in 1790 he overstrained himself on a marathon walk from Glasgow to Orkney. He never fully recovered and was a semi-invalid for some years before his death.

GEDDES (Nairn). *See* Rose, Hugh.

GIB, Adam. *See* Whitefield, George.

GILES [Egidius] *fl. c.* 700. Saint Giles' Cathedral, or the High Kirk of Edinburgh, has already enough good guidebooks, and its history is sufficiently well-known, to excuse its omission here. But many people ask 'Who is this Giles, and why is he remembered in a church which more appropriately would be "Saint Andrew's" or "Saint Columba's"?' Giles, in Latin Egidius, was a French hermit living near Arles, of doubtful date but probably dying *c.* 720. Born in Athens, he sought solitude in the west, first in Spain, then in France. His retreat was burnt by invading Muslims and he found refuge at Orleans under the protection of the powerful Charles Martel. His symbol is an arrow and he is often shown carrying a hind. The legend is that a hind he domesticated for its milk was pursued by hunters; he picked it up and was himself wounded by the arrow. He is associated with healing, especially of cripples. In London the church of Saint Giles' Cripplegate still stands, rebuilt after the blitz, and it may furnish the reason why our Saint Giles' acquired its name. Alexander I (1107–24) married Sybella, daughter of Henry I of England, whose queen, Matilda had founded a leper hospital in London, dedicated to Saint Giles. It seems natural that the Scottish queen might follow this example, especially as at the time there was a popular cult of the saint, brought over by crusaders who had seen the veneration in which he was held in France, and as her husband was at the time building a new church in Edinburgh. Saint Giles' Church, Elgin was also built about 1180 or 1200, and there was a fair in honour of the saint at Moffat.

GILFILLAN, George. 1813–78. Born at Comrie, Perthshire, son of a secession minister, became a secession minister himself and married the daughter of a neighbouring secession minister. At Glasgow University he was a fellow-student of Archbishop Tait† and later he continued studies at Edinburgh under Professor Wilson — more celebrated as the literary 'Christopher North' than as a teacher of philosophy. Gilfillan began writing early and it may be some of the professor's love of literature and literary expression had rubbed off on his pupil. In 1836 he went as minister to the secession congregation of School Wynd, Dundee, where he remained all his life. He had a huge literary output of pamphlets, essays, criticism and editions of poets. His edition of Burns is famous and still very readable is his *Gallery of Literary Portraits*. While he met and knew many well-known literary figures he tended to exaggerate his friendship with them. In spite of the fame which soon came to him from his writings, Gilfillan did not neglect his church and his people. He was always willing to help needy churches by giving one of his famous lectures on some literary theme and he brought well-known figures such as Emerson to speak at the local Mechanics' Institute, of which he was a keen supporter. In church matters he wrote in favour of a freer interpretation of the doctrinal standards and he was a keen 'Voluntary', disliking any State connection. He married but left no children. On his death the procession to the grave on the slope of Balgay cemetery was over two miles long. Today the massive memorial which his friends erected over the grave still stands, looking over a city from which his School Wynd has been swept away and where his manse, once hospitable to many famous figures, is now in danger of demolition. His successor in School Wynd, David MacRae (descendant of John Barclay's† successor at the Berean meeting-house) was expelled from the United Presbyterian Church (to which the congregation now belonged) because of certain objections he had to the Westminster Confession. He and many followers left and founded an independent congregation which still exists today as the Gilfillan Memorial, retaining many of its presbyterian features and not part of the Scottish Congregational Union.

GILLESPIE CHURCH, DUNFERMLINE.

Mother Church of the branch of presbyterianism known as The Relief, now within the Church of Scotland. After Thomas Gillespie† was deposed he ministered in the little meeting-house in Chapel Street, Dunfermline, purchased for his use by friends. There was sympathy with him and for the stand he had taken far outwith the immediate district, and others with their own grievances against the Established Church took courage. In Jedburgh, controversy centred on Thomas Boston, son of the famous 'Marrow' theologian (see note on Ettrick) and himself minister first at Ettrick, then at Oxnam. In 1755 the people of Jedburgh desired to call him, but the Crown as patron presented another. The 'sin of schism' had never greatly troubled Presbyterians and in those days it

was more possible financially to build and run an Independent meeting-house. Dunfermline had set the pattern. A chapel was built and the Jedburgh magistrates so approved that they had the town bells rung and walked to the new chapel in procession. Gillespie himself took no part but he was called upon to assist in the second Sacrament season. In 1761 a similar case occurred at Kilconquhar, Fife, where a new chapel was erected at Colinsburgh after consulting Mr Gillespie about the steps they should take. At Jedburgh Boston had been preached in by an English Presbyterian and Colinsburgh called another — Thomas Colier of Ravenstondale, Westmorland, — as minister. Immediately following Colier's induction Boston, Gillespie and he constituted themselves a presbytery to be known as the Presbytery of Relief. Gavin Struthers, historian of that body, writes 'the new presbytery became a rallying point for suffering parishes — they fled like doves to their windows'. First to seek admittance to the new body was Blairlogie (1762), followed by Auchtermuchty and, in the west, Bellshill. The first Edinburgh congregation was College Street. At its peak the Relief numbered about 60 congregations and 36,000 members mainly in the central belt of Scotland. It kept fairly closely to Gillespie's ideas of a Church: Presbyterian, but with little real presbyterial authority over individual congregations; open communion as far as possible with other Protestant bodies; open-mindedness to new ideas such as the introduction of hymns; separation of Church from State. In 1847, a century after its founding, the Relief Synod (by then with three presbyteries) united with the United Secession Church, or 'New Lichts' to form the United Presbyterian Church. On Thomas Gillespie's death his son Robert was not friendly to the Relief and when he proposed transferring the building back to the Church of Scotland, the majority of the members, in order to retain their Relief principles, crossed the road and erected a new chapel on the site now occupied by the congregation of the Church of Scotland named after Gillespie. The original site on the opposite side of the road became a chapel-of-ease, later St Andrew's Parish Church and recently united with Erskine

Church, one of the Original Secession congregations.

GILLESPIE, Thomas. 1708–74. Born in Duddingston parish, brought up by his widowed mother, who (writes Gavin Struthers, the 'Relief' historian) 'from the abundant resources of a mother's love had recourse to authoritative and pointed means to impress his heart with the necessity of being born again.' She used to make the long journey to Ettrick† for Boston's Sacrament sessions, and when she introduced her son to the great preacher 'a visible change immediately ensued', indicating that the minister's spiritual contact succeeded where the mother's 'pointed means' had failed. He began divinity studies in Edinburgh but when his mother joined the Seceders he enrolled in their 'hall' under Wilson of Perth. He stayed with them only ten days, repelled by their exclusiveness and their harking back to the old Covenants. He went south and joined the academy of Dr Doddridge at Northampton who had a deep influence on his life. Back in Scotland in 1741 he was presented to Carnock near Dunfermline. He might have remained a useful parish minister all his life but for the one unfortunate incident which was over-dramatized and resulted in his suspension. In a vacancy at Inverkeithing an English Dissenter, William Adams, was chosen by the people, but the minister of Broughton, Andrew Richardson, was presented by the patron. Feeling over such presentations ran high and the Assembly determined to uphold what was the law of the land. Gillespie and some others refused to share in the induction and he was chosen as the scapegoat to suffer deposition. No one has suggested that Gillespie was associated with the English Dissenter, but undoubtedly he had many friends from his Northamptonshire days and was therefore suspect; it was obvious that his sympathies were not whole-heartedly with the Establishment. 'I am no longer minister of Carnock' he said bitterly to his wife as she met him on his return to the manse. 'If we must beg,' she replied, 'I will carry the meal-poke.' Whitefield's† comment was 'The Pope has turned presbyterian' and Gillespie never again occupied his pulpit. On the next

Sabbath he preached in a field, announcing Psalm 73 before taking as text 1 Cor. 9: 16. Many wanted him to set up a dissenting chapel in Carnock parish but he was forestalled by the Seceders who set up theirs at Cairneyhill. His followers obtained a building in Dunfermline (*see* note on Gillespie Church) and he preached there till his death, watching the growth of the Relief, the new denomination which he had involuntarily founded.

GILLIES, John. *See* Wesley, John.

GLAS, John. 1695–1773. Born Auchtermuchty, ordained to Tealing (Angus) he soon rethought his doctrine of the Church, and concluded that: (*a*) no idea of a National Church could be found in the New Testament; (*b*) there was no scriptural authority for the Covenants, nor should any magistrate have any function in the Church; (*c*) the Church should be a spiritual society consisting only of true believers who had experienced a sense of saving grace. Presbyterial superintendence cannot have been strict, for Glas continued for a time as parish minister while he also founded and supervised an independent congregation of about 100 adherents who accepted his tenets. In 1728 he was deposed

John Glas

by the Synod of Angus and Mearns and removed to Dundee where he set up a second congregation in a small octagonal building adjoining St Andrew's Church — a building now considered of sufficient architectural interest to have a part in the redeveloped town. Seeking to recapture the polity of the early Church he decided that each congregation should have a 'plurality of elders or presbyters' (*see* note on David Dale) and he was joined in this office at Dundee by Mr Archibald, minister at Guthrie. Education, or knowledge of the Bible tongues was not considered necessary for the Glasite 'ministry'. In 1736 he was joined by Robert Sandeman, elder in the Perth Church and Glas's son-in-law, who shared with him leadership of a rapidly expanding denomination. In England and in America, which Sandeman visited, they are often known as Sandemanians. During the interval between the Sabbath services it was the Glasite custom to hold an 'agape' or fellowship meal, and this led to the derisory title of the 'Kail Kirk' as large quantities of vegetables were boiled to make soup. The iron pump by which the Dundee Glasites obtained their water is at present being preserved by St Andrew's Church. They had weekly Communion and very soon a hymnal, *Christian Songs*, was introduced. Not only the large towns in Scotland had Glasite Churches but small places like Leslie, Cupar, Dunkeld and Galashiels. There were also several units in England and America. The denomination stood midway between Presbyterianism and Congregationalism in polity. John Glas was the first to see the possibility of a Church existing without State recognition or support. His followers were often treated with less respect than they deserved as many of their leaders were men of little education. They have been accused of lack of charity and narrow-mindedness which some have attributed rather to Sandeman than to Glas. There must have been many good points in a sect which attracted and included the scientist Michael Faraday, who worshipped in the London group at St Martins-le-Grand and is said to have attended service in the Dundee church while he was in the town giving a lecture at the Mechanics Institute. A well-known Scottish journalist who died recently often spoke of his mother's simple and devout life as a Sandemanian. The sect is not yet dead; descendants of Sandeman maintain the worship in a small hall in Edinburgh. Glas is buried in Dundee Howff. *See also* Keiss.

GLASGOW, Sixth Earl of. *See* Cumbrae.

GLENALMOND (Perthshire). *See* Cumbrae; Dowden, John; Wordsworth, Charles.

GLENDEVON (Perthshire). *See* Serf.

GLENFINNAN (Argyll). *See* Macdonald, Hugh.

GLEN URQUHART [Tober Churadain] (Inverness-shire). *See* Curitan.

GOBRIAT (Invergowrie). *See* Curitan.

GORDON, Catherine, of Gordonstoun. *See* Barclay, Robert.

GORDON, Charles. 1772–1855. Known throughout Aberdeen and the north-east as Priest Gordon. Born at Bellie (Banffshire), he entered Scalan Seminary† and continued studies at the French college of Douai. Because of the danger on the outbreak of the French Revolution the Scottish students for the priesthood had to make a hurried return in 1793 and he was back at Scalan for another two years. The old seminary was at the time being replaced by the new college at Aquhorties but the young priest left for St Peter's, Aberdeen where after 3 years he became priest-in-charge, a position he held till his death 57 years later. A new St Peter's was built in the fashionable Gothic style and opened in 1804. Mr Gordon — note that the title 'Father' was reserved at that time for 'regulars' and 'secular priests' were simply addressed as 'Mister' until comparatively recent times — was well known for his broad Banffshire accent which he employed even in the pulpit. It was said that as a young priest he had been rebuked for this by his bishop (James Kyle) and in the broadest dialect replied 'Weel, bishop, jest ye spier at ony o' ma bairns the questions o' their catechis an if they dinna gie ye the correct answer I'll change ma language.' He took particular care over the instruction of his people, with 'Christian Doctrine' every Sunday at 2.30 followed by a catechetical lecture. Music had had little place in Scottish Catholicism but he introduced music at the second of his two Sunday masses, and High Mass was celebrated at the opening of St Peter's a rare event in Scotland at the time.

GORDON, Jean, Countess of Perth. *See* Stobhall.

GORDONSTOUN (Moray). *See* Barclay, Robert.

GOVAN. *See* Constantine.

GRACEHILL (Co. Antrim). *See* Caldwell, John.

GRANGE CEMETERY, EDINBURGH. *See* Agnew, Andrew; Chalmers, Thomas; Lee, Robert; Miller, Hugh.

GRANT, James. *See* Hay, George.

GREENOCK. *See* Struthers, James P.

GREYFRIARS KIRK, EDINBURGH. Unlike monks, whose cloisters were usually built at some distance from the centres of population, friars were preaching orders whose friaries were always in the middle of the burghs whose people they were to serve. One result has been that we have scarcely any remains of mediaeval friaries; the value of the ground was so great that it was quickly used for other purposes after the Reformation. Both at Dundee and in Edinburgh it was used for burial purposes, but in the latter case the higher part became the site of a new church to serve the south-west area of the town. Greyfriars Church was opened on Christmas Day 1620 and the entry was by the steep path or causey from the Cowgate. The many illustrations of the National Covenant being signed in the kirkyard on the tombstones are only partially correct; it was signed first in the Magdalen Chapel† and in the church itself before the common folk signed their copies in the open air. During Cromwell's occupation of the town, Greyfriars was used as barracks, while the adjoining Heriot's Hospital, not yet opened as a charity school, became the infirmary

Greyfriars Kirk, Edinburgh

E

fo.· 'ye sick sodgers'. In 1656 a wall was erected to divide the church into two but was removed after six years. The advantage of two smaller kirks was not lost sight of, however, for when the tower at the west end blew up in 1718 — it had been used by the Town Council for storing gunpowder — the opportunity was taken to add a new church to the west of the old one. The two churches existed back to back until 1938, although Old Greyfriars had been badly burned and largely rebuilt during the ministry of Dr Lee† in 1845. In 1938 a very worthy restoration made it into one seemly place for Presbyterian worship. An authority on post-Reformation churches (George Hay) describes it as 'a rather solid structure with a certain dour dignity'. Among congregations later absorbed into Greyfriars were the old parish of Lady Yester's and the former U.F. New North. The graveyard is even more interesting than the church. Part was used as a prison for Covenanters from Bothwell Brig, there is a large Martyrs' Monument and a huge tomb for 'Bloody Mackenzie' their persecutor, as well as many graves from Edinburgh's 'Golden Age' — providing an epitome of Scotland's post-Reformation history. There is also, of course, the tradition of the world-famous dog, Bobby, who probably draws more visitors to Greyfriars than all its historical associations.

GRIERSON, Sir Robert, of Lag. *See* Balmaghie Church.

GUINEVERE. *See* Meigle.

GUTHRIE, Thomas. 1803–73. Born at Brechin, he was descended from two famous Covenanting ministers: James Guthrie, who was executed for disowning the royal authority in 1661, and William Guthrie, chaplain to the Scots army at Dunbar, and on his mother's side from a staunch seceding family. He entered Edinburgh University at the early age of 12 and was there ten years, studying not only Arts and Divinity, but Chemistry, Natural Science and Anatomy — the last under Dr Knox of body-snatching fame. Licensed in 1825, he despaired of securing a parish as he was already marked as an Evangelical while most livings were in the hands of the Moderates, so he set off for Paris to study

medicine and science. After two years he returned to Scotland, supplied pulpits and even for a time acted as a bank manager. Then in 1830 the Hon. William Maule, heritor of Arbirlot, near Arbroath, offered him the living. During his ministry there an outbreak of cholera proved the usefulness of his medical knowledge. Throughout his life his scientific training made him more practical than many of his brethren and attracted to his Edinburgh congregation men like J. Y. Simpson, Hugh Miller and Professor Blackie. After serving his country charge for eight years Guthrie was called to the collegiate charge of Old Greyfriars but the shadow of disruption was clouding Scottish church life and in 1843 he, with many of his members, left to form Free St John's. He became the most eloquent pleader for the 'manse fund' of the new denomination, travelling widely to make appeals. Guthrie's manse was in Salisbury Road and it was while he was one day walking in the King's Park near St Antony's Well that two urchins offered him a drink for a halfpenny. He found they had never attended school. 'Would you go to school if, beside your learning, you were to get breakfast, dinner and supper there?' he asked. 'It would have done any man's heart good,' he wrote 'to have seen the flash of joy that broke from the eyes of one of them . . . The boy leapt to his feet. "Aye, will I sir, and bring the haill land [the whole tenement] wi' me."' So the idea of 'Ragged Schools' was born in Guthrie's mind. He was not the pioneer in this for Dundee and Aberdeen already had schools for destitute children and other schemes were afoot, but Guthrie had the eloquence and zeal to make the idea appeal to the public, and also the organizing capacity to work it to a practical shape. In 1847 the boys' school was opened with seven pupils and the girls' with thirteen. From the original conception of Ragged Schools: to feed the children, keep them from mischief and give them a modicum of learning, the aim changed to that of 'Industrial Schools' to turn the energy of those who might have become members of the criminal class into honest hard-working artisans. Bible teaching was part, but by no means a major part, of the curriculum. On occasion this led to difficulty with the Roman Catholic authorities who desired religious teaching to be kept separate. While Guthrie disavowed any intention of his schools being denominational he held to his original position and while many Catholic children continued to pass through his schools there was a rival movement, 'The United Industrial Schools'. Thackeray called the ragged schools 'the finest sight in Edinburgh'. After many changes the two original schools became Approved Schools for boys and for girls, a title now changed officially to 'List D Schools'. Guthrie was buried in Grange Cemetery and is commemorated by a large statue in Princes Street. His church, St John's, had a curious fate when, as part of the property settlement of 1905, it was awarded to the minority for their Assembly Hall and for the evicted congregation of St Columba's Gaelic Church, who renamed Guthrie's church after their former home. In this new role it has seen the notable ministries of Donald Maclean, Alexander Stewart and G. N. M. Collins. It still houses the 'Opposition Assembly' 'across the road' from that of the Church of Scotland.

HACKET, Andrew. *See* Stobhall.

HADDINGTON. *See* Brown, John; Irving, Edward; Knox, John; Mylne, Andrew.

HALDANE, Robert (1764–1842) and **James** (1768–1851). Both the Baptists and the Congregationalists in Scotland look back on the Haldane brothers almost as founding-fathers. They were of the Gleneagles family which has produced a notable succession of scholars, scientists, soldiers and national leaders. After a short period at Dundee High School the brothers received most of their education by lodging in Charles Street, Edinburgh with the famous Dr Adam of the High School. Both entered the navy but Robert left at the age of 20, attended Edinburgh University classes, married and would have settled down as laird of his new estate of Airthrey (*see* note on Logie Airth) but for the influence of the French Revolution which imprinted liberal ideas on him and — more important — a deep religious experience which demanded, eventually, the selling of much of his property and the employment of his wealth in a variety of Christian social

projects. These included the sending of a mission to Bengal (which was blocked by the government), the setting up of a college for laymen-preachers, and — most notable and most expensive — the building of several huge preaching-houses called Tabernacles. James had his conversion experience when in the navy. He returned to Edinburgh where he was influenced by a lay-preacher, John Campbell, who worked in the Grassmarket among the poorest classes. Unlike his elder brother, who preached little and never became a minister, James became an active evangelist, organizing from 1797 onwards a series of preaching tours which took him and his band of loyal followers throughout Scotland, especially to the remotest districts of the Highlands, Neither brother cared much for denominational allegiance; they found the established church too formal and do not seem to have seriously considered any of the presbyterian alternatives, being more attracted to English Non-conformity and Independency. James was ordained and took charge of the parent tabernacle in Edinburgh. It was inevitable that tensions would rise in what was virtually the creation of a new denomination, and three of these can be traced: (*a*) between a settled ministry and the original conception of visiting evangelists; (*b*) between the idea of a congregation with a minister supported by a group of 'elders' or 'deacons' very like a presbyterian kirk-session, or a number of equal ruling presbyters, one of which might be employed full-time (*see* note on David Dale); and (*c*) between infant baptism and believers' baptism with immersion. In 1808 James openly declared for adult baptism and the movement began to divide, with Greville Ewing† leading those who opposed the Haldanes on this point. After the division, membership of the Edinburgh Tabernacle fell by two thirds but this was largely due to other causes — it had departed from the original idea of a preaching station for the unchurched and become just another congregation with its own people and its own minister. Other schemes of Robert's had not been very successful or had been abandoned, such as his idea of bringing the children of Indian chiefs to be educated and converted in Scotland; he was also wasting a great deal of effort on wrangling with the Bible Societies about the inclusion of the apocryphal books in their bibles. The most lasting effects of the Haldane movement have been in the more remote parts of Scotland, particularly in the Highlands, where there are still active units of the Baptist or Congregationalist persuasion who trace directly back to James Haldane's missionary tours.

HALLIDAY, David. *See* Balmaghie Church.

HAMILTON, Patrick. 1504–28. There is some doubt about Hamilton's exact birth-place. He was high-born, related to the Duke of Albany and so at the age of 14 he was made 'Commendator' or titular-Abbot of Fearn in Ross-shire. He was educated at St Andrews and early was suspected of liberal views. For commending the Tyn-dale Bible he was charged with heresy in 1526 but escaped to Marburg where he met Luther. He composed the *Loci Communes*, known as 'Patrick's Pleas' in which he set forth the doctrine of justifica-tion by faith. In 1527 he returned to Scot-land where, within a year, he was seized, tried and burned outside the gateway of St Salvator's College. The traditional spot is marked on the cobblestones. His connec-tion with the small Premonastratensian Abbey of Fearn lasted only until 1525 and can have been no more than nominal but he is commemorated by a plaque in the nearby parish church of Tain.

HANBY, Thomas. *See* Dall, Robert.

HARVIESTOUN (Clackmannanshire). *See* Mylne, Andrew; Tait, Archibald.

HAY, George. 1729–1811. Bishop and Vicar-Apostolic of the Lowland Area. In the days of the penal laws, before the res-toration of the Scottish Roman Catholic dioceses, the country was administered for a time through two vicars-apostolic of the 'Scottish mission' with the dividing line roughly from Inverness to Bute. The future Bishop Hay came of a strongly Jacobite, non-juring family in the Episcopal Church; his father had been imprisoned and ban-ished after the 1715. Born in Edinburgh, he was apprenticed to an Edinburgh surgeon and was among students who helped to tend the wounded after Prestonpans. He

Bishop George Hay

followed the Prince's army into England. Illness forced his return but for the small part he had played in the Rising he was imprisoned for three months in Edinburgh and then for a further year in London. Here he first turned to the Roman Church and took the final step of becoming a Catholic in 1748 at the age of 19. His student friend ,'Lang Sandy' Wood, later a well-known Edinburgh surgeon, exclaimed, 'Weel, Geordie, ye're a damn fule for yer pains in becoming a popish priest — ye wad hae made a damn guid doctor'. As his adopted religion would bar him from graduating at the university or taking his diploma at the College of Surgeons, Hay took a post as ship's surgeon, and while in London, he met and became a lifelong friend of the saintly Bishop Challoner through whose influence he decided on the priesthood. He studied at the Scots College, Rome, was priested by Cardinel Spinelli and landed back in Scotland in secret with his fellow-students Geddes and Guthrie at Buckhaven. Mr Hay found that in spite of his 'turning' his family welcomed him. In 1759 he was appointed priest at Rathven in the Enzie of Banffshire, a strongly Catholic district (pronounce with the Scots 'z' as 'y' in the traditional way, i.e.

'Eenyie', with soft 'g' sound). During this period he resided with Bishop Grant at Preshome, a place which had long associations with the clergy. Here he restored the little Chapel of the Craigs which had been destroyed after the '45. Even in this spot, remote and hidden in a wooded defile, secrecy had to be maintained. In his lengthy correspondence with Mr Geddes†, who later became his coadjutor bishop, a secret code was used: Rome and the Pope were 'Hilltown' and 'The old gentleman', the bishop was 'the physician' and communicants were 'the customers'. In 1769 Hay returned to Edinburgh, soon to be appointed coadjutor bishop, and vicar-apostolic of the Lowland District nine years later. In Edinburgh he opened two chapels: in Blackfriars Wynd and Leith Wynd. In 1778 he took a leading part in the abortive attempt to have the Scottish penal laws repealed. His own house was sacked while he watched from the opposite pavement. After 1788, as his health failed, he retired to Scalan† where he cared for the students, transferring with them to the new seminary at Aquhorties. His work in the wider church had ceased; he was referred to kindly as 'our careworn superior and father', but his influence over the boys and the young priests was at its greatest. The strictness for which he had been noted mellowed, and he loved to have them round him as he told stories of his own part in the now distant Jacobite rising. Death came quietly to him at the age of 83.

HAYMARKET STATION, EDINBURGH. *See* Burns, William C.

HEAVENFIELD (Northumberland). *See* Aidan.

HENDERSON, Alexander. *See* Leuchars.

HENRYSON, Josina. *See* Sciennes.

HEPBURN, John. *c.* 1649–1723. Founder and leader of the Hebronites, who after the Revolution of 1689 hovered on the borders of the Established Church, claiming its stipends and privileges but rejecting its authority and discipline. Their text-book (not written by Hepburn himself) was appropriately titled *Humble Pleadings for the Good Old Ways*. They are often confused with the Cameronians but were not so extreme, although they collected a list of 26 grievances against Church and State. Like the Hillmen they were organized in 'societies'. Hepburn's career may be best viewed as a life-long series of controversies and confrontations. Galen would have typed him as 'choleric', modern psychologists as a 'hyper-thyroid'; Daniel Defoe, who met him, dubbed him 'mad'; Veitch, minister of Dumfries, called him a rascal. Hepburn held opinions very strongly, but sometimes it was not clear which opinions he held, as when he gathered 600 followers in arms at the time of the 1715 Rising and marched them on Dumfries without revealing whether they were to fight for or against the Jacobites. He was accused of 'joucking' (vacillating) but he showed considerable personal courage in the days of the conventicles, preaching fearlessly from Moray down to the borders. He was a powerful preacher, drawing people to his church from a radius of 25 miles — even Veitch admitted 'he had a way of couping folk'. It was recorded that on one occasion he preached and prayed in public for seven hours at a stretch. He was rather irregularly called to the parish of Urr before the Revolution, and later was three times suspended or deposed for contumacy and refusing to submit to the Courts of the Church. He continued to function, disregarding all the verdicts and for a time he also ministered in the neighbouring parish of Kirkgunzeon. He was deeply involved in the Galloway rising against the 1707 Union, but it was suspected that he was also informing for the unionists. In 1712, when an Oath of Allegiance was demanded of parish ministers he refused to take it. When the Jacobites began to prepare for the 1715 Rising, he collected his followers and drilled them on Halmyre Hill at Urr. As the laird, Maxwell of Munches, was a prominent Catholic who was later taken prisoner at Preston, it would seem that the Hebronites were expected to support his cause. They marched out behind a yellow banner inscribed FOR THE LORD OF HOSTS — a sufficiently ambiguous motto. On the collapse of the Rising they speedily disbanded and Hepburn declared he had never been a Jacobite. Some of his followers joined the 'Levellers' who in 1720 pulled down the new land enclosures.

HICKHORNGILL, Edward. *fl. c.* 1650. Little is known of this Baptist pastor, but he may be taken to represent the brief time during the Commonwealth when the germ of a Baptist Church took root in Scotland, only to wither and disappear for a time under the persecution which followed the Restoration. In 1652 Major-general Lillburne had encouraged the formation of a Baptist meeting in Edinburgh and Leith; it is recorded that 'some were dippet at Bonnington Mill'. Those of Cromwell's troopers who were Baptists had with them their chaplains who found a response, although limited, among the Scots people. They sent south to Hexham for one Edward Hickhorngill to come to minister to them. Whatever happened is not known but the result of his attempt to minister to Scotsmen was to send him south 'a desperate atheist'. This phase of disbelief, which may have been exaggerated, must have passed for he was restored to communion at Hexham. General Monck, Cromwell's representative in Scotland, had little sympathy with the Baptist element in his army and actually imprisoned some Baptist officers in Tantallon Castle.

HIGH KIRK OF EDINBURGH (St Giles Cathedral). *See* Giles.

HINBA. *See* Aileach an Naoimh.

HODDOM (Dumfriesshire). *See* Kentigern.

HOGG, James (The Ettrick Shepherd). *See* Ettrick Kirk.

HOLLIS, Daniel. *See* Barclay, John.

HOLY TRINITY PARISH CHURCH, EDINBURGH. *See* Maxwell, Willielma.

HOPE, Lady Henrietta. *See* Maxwell, Willielma.

HOPE, John. 1807–93. Writer to the Signet; his father, James (son of Dr Hope the founder of the new Edinburgh Botanical Gardens) had attended the High School with Walter Scott and John also was educated there. All his life was spent in the New Town of Edinburgh, as a boy at 65 Queen Street and later at his own home and business address, 31 Moray Place. He is remembered as the apostle of the Total Abstinence movement in Scotland, but he also protested against smoking tobacco, snuff, billiards, horse-racing, gambling, Sunday trains, hunting, ritual, 'liturgy', and especially 'Popery' in any form. For 30 years he abstained from tea and coffee as they were artificial stimulants. He was, however, very fond of oranges, football and military music. As he was a bachelor and lived extremely frugally, he acquired a large fortune which he gave to found The Hope Trust, devoted to furthering the many causes dear to his heart. In these changed days it is difficult to take John Hope seriously. To us he is so often fanatical, as when he boasts that when on the outside seat of a coach to Pitlochry, he lectured his fellow travellers so fiercely that when passing Dunkeld one emptied his snuff box overboard, while soon after the other threw his pipe over into the River Bran; or when he voted for the opening of Princes Street Gardens to the public only on condition that large 'no smoking' notices were erected at each entrance. At the height of the Catholic enfranchisement controversy he opened a 'No Popery Sunday School' in Leith. When the city was threatened with cholera he advocated a new railway station near the Grassmarket so that young people from the slums might be transported en masse to Granton to bathe and wash. These were his more extreme efforts and it is these which are remembered more vividly than the many very sensible schemes which he supported when he was on the Town Council or the School Board: better housing, a more sensible educational system, a playing park at Stockbridge or a bathing pool at the east end of the Meadows. This last only came to pass after many years as a mere paddling pond while the Stockbridge park disappeared under housing. He assisted many young men to become ministers, of whom the most notable was the vigorous anti-catholic propagandist, Jacob Primmer†. Hope remained a loyal member of the Established Church in spite of getting little support from it for many of his cherished reforms.

HUME, Alexander. *See* Logie Airth.

HUME, Sir Patrick. *See* Baillie, Lady Grisell (1).

HUNTER, John. 1848–1917. Minister of Trinity Congregational Church, Glasgow, from 1886 to 1901 and again from 1904 to 1913. He compiled and published a service book which became a model for liturgical or 'high-church' Non-conformist congregations, and the service at Trinity, with sung responses, chants and good music, attracted university students and large congregations of west-end citizens to this beautiful sanctuary. Between his two ministries at Trinity he established a similar liturgical tradition at King's Weigh House, London, later to be continued under the famous Dr Orchard who eventually became a Roman Catholic. Hunter took a very liberal standpoint in theology and also established at Trinity a reputation for social consciousness which was maintained by his successors.

HUNTLY. *See* Macdonald, George; Rainy, Robert.

INCHKENNETH (Isle of Mull). *See* Kenneth.

INCHMAHOME PRIORY (Stirlingshire; AM). A motor-boat transports visitors across the Lake of Menteith to the delightful ruins of this secluded priory of Augustinian or Black Canons. They were not monks but 'canons regular', combining the 'regular' or disciplined life with the active parish priesthood. The site is Celtic — Innis mo-Cholmaig — and derives from the Ulster saint Colman or Colmoc of Dromore†. The mediaeval community was founded in 1238 by Walter Comyn, Earl of Menteith. Bruce was a frequent visitor and Mary of Scots spent some time here in her childhood.

INDUSTRIAL BRIGADE HOME, TRONGATE, GLASGOW. *See* Quarrier, William.

INNES, Andrew. d. 1846. The most devoted and the longest lived of the sect founded by Elspeth Simpson, 'Luckie' Buchan†. Native of Muthill, mason to trade and such a zealous member of the Relief Church that he walked to Glasgow

Inchmahome Priory and Lake of Menteith

Andrew Innes the Buchanite

to attend the Sacrament. There he met Mrs Buchan, who on Glasgow Green expounded to him the prophetic revelation by which she was the woman in Revelation 12. She had great power of attraction for young people and soon Andrew left home to join the new sect at Irvine. When Mrs Buchan was badly hurt by the mob he took her in his cart to his parents' home in Perthshire to recover, and as a result several Muthill families became Buchanites. Although he was not an educated man, nor a clever one, it is to him we look for what little we know about the community. Undoubtedly part of their bad reputation comes from a self-righteous letter written by Robert Burns who knew them at Irvine and from rumours circulated by local ministers. Today their sharing society might be looked on more kindly. Innes became 'Friend Mother's' devoted helper and when they reached Closeburn he was sent back to Irvine to bring Jean Gardner, whose family had joined the sect. She had lingered behind, perhaps because she was in love with Burns — some critics believe that she, and not Jean Armour, was the 'Bonnie Jean' of his poem. Innes himself was in love with her sister Katie Gardner but one of the Buchanite tenets was no

marriage, no begetting of children as the end of things was imminent. Katie became pregnant and Friend Mother's wrath was great against them both. Andrew was at first excluded but later he and Katie were allowed to return on condition that they must never show any affection to the child who would be reared by the community; nor must they ever acknowledge each other as man and wife. The child was weakminded and, perhaps fortunately, died. Andrew and Katie kept their promise. On Mrs Buchan's death it was he who hid her body for over half a century, moving it as they moved. She had claimed that she would rise again after 50 years and on 29 March 1841 he was seen to be constantly watching the skies, taking warm blankets up to the closet where, his friends knew, the corpse was hidden. At nightfall he was a hopeless, broken man. Old Katie, who had long since ceased to believe, was the only other left. They still kept the promise of nonmarriage and treated each other as strangers although each spoke and acted kindly to the other. Her last words when, two years later she was dying, were 'Oh be carefu' o' Andrew, he sits wi' his feet on the ribs o' the grate, which has fashed me muckle . . . his legs micht be roasted afore he could shift his chair.' As he had requested, the mummified body of 'Luckie' Buchan was buried below his own at the back of the house in Crocketford. If Andrew had not chanced to meet Mrs Buchan in the Saltmarket of Glasgow he might have remained in his native village, to marry and beget a family and to die a respected elder of the Relief Church.

INNES, Margaret. *See* Rose, Hugh.

INNIS MEDCANT. *See* Lindisfarne.

INVERARAY   PARISH   CHURCH (Argyll). The present little burgh represents an eighteenth century town-plan designed by Robert Mylne, last of the royal Master-masons, at the commands of the fifth Duke of Argyll when he desired to remove the villagers to a respectful distance from his new castle. Mylne made the parish church the central feature of the community, placing it on an eminence and providing it with two fronts, one for the Gaelic or Highland and the other for the English, or Lowland, congregation. A cross-wall divided the interior into two rectangular churches over which a centrally placed and graceful spire presided. Today the need for the Gaelic part has gone and it is used as a church hall, while the remainder, the present parish kirk, may be viewed as an example of how terribly a seemly Georgian church can be mishandled by generations of Scots — ministers, elders, burgesses and nobles combined. When heavy traffic caused the spire to need attention in 1945 it was pulled down as dangerous and now that the deed is recognized for the iconoclasm it was, a fund is being gathered to put it up again. Internally, the simple classical dignity has been shattered by a heavy Italian style pulpit, a brass eagle lectern equally out of place, with a short and insignificant Communion Table sandwiched between. Above, an imitation clerestory throws light on the deserted laird's loft where the plush of the chair of Mac Cailein Mor is frayed and dusty. Much of the little burgh itself has been tastefully restored by the late Ian Lindsay.

INVERESK (Midlothian). *See* Carlyle, Alexander.

INVERGOWRIE (Angus). *See* Curitan.

INVERKEITHING (Fife). *See* Angus, John; Gillespie, Thomas.

INVERNESS. *See* Kenneth; MacLeod, John.

INVERURIE (Aberdeenshire). Here the rivers Don and Urie meet and it is in their valleys, for some unexplained reason, that we find the finest collection of Pictish symbol and animal stones. Most of the stones in this district are classed by archaeologists as Class 1, that is, they show one or more symbols but no Christian cross. They are most probably pre-Christian; usually they are huge, roughly shaped boulders with incised characters. Class 2, which are more common in Angus, show one or more of the usual symbols or animals and in addition a cross or Christian sign; often these are more regularly-cut slabs and the characters are in relief. In the Class 3, the pagan symbols have disappeared. Of Class 1 stones in the area good examples are in Port Elphinstone cemetery, with three

Class 1 stone — Logie Elphinstone

separate stones, at Kintore churchyard, Drimmies farm, a particularly massive example with ogham writing at Brandsbutt (AM), and along at Logie Elphinstone (now Logie House Hotel) another three stones, one with unique circular ogham and a symbol erased and recut by the Pictish sculptor. Nearby, at Chapel of Garioch (where the church is also worth a visit) stands the great Maiden Stone (AM), one of the best examples of a Class 2 stone with cross, and pagan symbols together. There have been several theories about the meaning of the animals and symbols of these stones, but none generally accepted. The same symbols cut in varieties of the same style include the inverted crescent, with its interior filled with design scrolls, the double disc, a cooking pot viewed from above, a wedge which may represent a chariot and, going with such symbols, a comb and mirror. A broken lance or a broken arrow accompany certain of the symbols. The animals include the boar, bull, wolf, serpent, fish, eagle and (quite different from the others) a very stylized 'elephant' with feet almost like wheels. Professor Thomas has suggested that the stones are in most cases memorial stones, erected by widow or mother (the comb and mirror) to a king or sub king, or high official (discs, crescent, etc.) of a bull, wolf or other animal tribe. It is clear that whatever their meaning the original pre-Christian symbols did not give offence when the tribe was Christianized as they saw no incongruity in placing the cross and the elephant or other symbol on two sides of the same stone or even beside each other.

IONA, Isle of (Argyll). The name by which this island is universally known in English perpetuates an error, for the 'n' is really a 'u' which became inverted, giving a word which in Hebrew means 'a dove' — appropriate as the saint who was to give it fame himself bore the Latin name for the same bird. IOUA is an adjective — the practice in Adamnan and other mediaeval Latin writers was to use the noun 'insula' with an appropriate adjective when describing an island — and the corresponding noun is I or Y (pronounced 'ee'), or sometimes Eo, Yi, or Hii. Usually in Scots or Irish Gaelic it is coupled with the saint's name, Icolmkill, or more fully, I-chaluim-cille. (*See* the note on Columba.) The island has accumulated more than its share of doubtful 'historical' facts, which provoke the following comments:

(*a*) No one in his right senses would try to land a currough at Columba Bay when there is a reasonable landing place where the jetty is now.

(*b*) There is little evidence for the story that Columba sailed via Oronsay and Colonsay. Most likely he kept east of Kintyre both for safer sailing and to call on his Dalriadic king at Dunadd.

(*c*) The popular story of the 'Hill with its back to Ireland' (Cairn Cul ri Eareann) which he is supposed to have climbed on landing and so named when he could no longer see his homeland, loses its point when we discover that just across in Mull stands another of the same name and also a 'Hill with its back to Scotland'.

(*d*) It is likely that Iona was a Christian centre before Columba landed. One MS tells of seven bishops already in occupation.

(*e*) It is unlikely that Iona would be chosen deliberately as the spearpoint for evangelization of the mainland; it is too remote. Lismore would be a better centre and there is some evidence that Columba

wanted it but was beaten to it by Moluag.

None of this detracts from the wonderful, even mystical, atmosphere of sancity which haunts the island. This seems to be in no way due to the Benedictine monks or the Augustinian nuns, pious and holy as they may possibly have been; nor, certainly, to later visitors like Johnson, Boswell or Prince Albert; but solely to the Celtic settlement in and after Columba's day. The actual abbey building was given to the Church of Scotland by the 8th Duke of Argyll and restored at the turn of the century; the monastic buildings have been restored since the last War by the Iona Community. Until Professor Thomas excavated a few years ago it was thought that the Celtic muinntir lay half a mile to the north of the mediaeval abbey, but he traced the 'rath' or boundary roughly to the limit of the present grounds, and pinpointed the site of the Ab's cell right on Tor Ab — the spot where Dr Macleod, leader of the Community, used to stand while he recited the sacred history to visitors. It may be called either 'Abbey' or 'Cathedral', for the Benedictine monastery later became the seat of the Bishop of the Isles.

IRVINE. *See* Robertson, W. B.; Simpson, Elspeth.

IRVING, Edward. 1792–1834. Born in Annan, he preceded Thomas Carlyle to the local Academy. He tutored little Jane Welsh, the doctor's daughter in Haddington, where he became schoolmaster before going on to a similar post at Kirkcaldy. In both places he was known for his strict discipline and for his taste in clothes, which included a tartan waistcoat. He became assistant to Dr Chalmers in Glasgow and in 1822 was called to the Scots charge in London which bore the strange title of the Caledonian Asylum's Chapel in Hatton Garden. It is probable that Irving had been in love with his former pupil, Jane, now grown to a young woman, but the minister of Kirkcaldy threatened to hold him to a supposed engagement to his daughter Isabella Martin. Thomas Carlyle, whom Irving had introduced to both Haddington and Kirkcaldy, married Jane, who, as subsequent events indicated, might well have been happier with the tall, handsome young minister with the black locks and attractive cast of eye. In London, society, politicians, even royalty had fallen to Irving's charms and lionized him. Within two years he and his office-bearers were building a new church in the fashionable Regent Square. He was a first-rate scholar with several volumes to his credit and a sound yet eloquent preacher; he held a very high view of the ministry and of the Church — yet within eight years he was deposed by the Presbytery of Annan which had originally licensed him. It was the most dramatic heresy case in the history of the Church of Scotland. The nominal charge was theological: on the nature of Christ's humanity: did He share fully man's corrupt nature? Everyone knew, however, that the real cause was Irving's Pentecostalism. He had become a member of the Albury circle which consisted of ministers from the Anglican, Baptist and other churches, Millenarians and Pentecostalists, seeking to revive speaking with tongues and prophesy. Irving accepted the interruption of church services, but his office-bearers strongly objected. In the end he was barred from the building. Regent Square later became the headquarters of the English Presbyterian Church. It was blitzed during the War and lay derelict for some years before rebuilding, with a plaster head detached from a bust of Irving left lying grotesquely on the floor. The Albury group, led by Henry Drummond, J. B. Cardale and others were organizing a new Pentecostal church, the Catholic Apostolic, often called Irvingites. But he was by no means their leader, though he was one of their leading thinkers. When deposed from the Church of Scotland he was given no higher rank in the new denomination than that of Angel, or Pastor, to the church in Newman Street, not far from his former charge. Much of what A. L. Drummond calls the 'paltry sacerdotalism' of Albury was quite alien to Irving's Presbyterian tradition and it is impossible not to conclude that he died of a broken heart when he realized the mistake he had made. Irving was on friendly terms with his fellow innovators in theology, McLeod Campbell† and Erskine of Linlathen†, but failed to persuade them to follow his Pentecostalism.

JEDBURGH. *See* Gillespie Church; Restenneth.

JEFFREYS, George. *See* City Temple.

JOCELYN OF FURNESS. *See* Kentigern.

JOHN KNOX CHURCH, GLASGOW. *See* Macfarlane, Donald.

JOLLY, Alexander. 1756–1838. Bishop of Moray and Episcopal minister at Fraserburgh: it would be difficult to decide which of the offices was to him the more important. Born at Stonehaven, the centre of a very Episcopally loyal district, he was educated at Aberdeen, tutored for a short time then took up the charge at Fraserburgh which he held for the rest of his life. It was an uneventful life but one looked back upon with affection by all Episcopalians who still speak of their Church in pre-Tractarian days as being 'in the times of Bishop Jolly'. He was never much of a diocesan Bishop but more on the lines of the early 'chorepiscopoi' or the Bishops of the Columban church, guarding zealously and administering carefully those functions he considered essentially episcopal but showing no desire to rule over or interfere with his fellow clergy. He despised titles such as 'my Lord' and was very content to use the word 'minister'. His clerical dress and his form of service was much more akin to the Presbyterian than to the modern Episcopalian. His personal life was equally simple; he remained a bachelor, living in a two-storied house on the main street of Fraserburgh. On the occasion of George IV's visit to Edinburgh his fellow bishops were apprehensive of the impression the Bishop of Moray might create as his clothes were out-of-date in style and his wig was threadbare. However, he was presented with a new wig and took care to make the correct motions and so won the regard of the Hanoverian — at a time when Scottish bishops were still looked upon as Jacobites. Jolly was High Tory in politics and in church he opposed every change in practice and procedure and avoided every convocation and conference he possibly could.

JONES, Thomas. *See* Ewing, Greville; Maxwell, Willielma.

KAMES (Argyllshire). *See* MacLeod, John.

KEISS (Caithness). Sir William Sinclair of Dunbeath, who had himself been baptized in adulthood in London, founded a meeting of Baptists here in 1750. They met at first in a vaulted room in his old castle. His tenets were like those of John Glas† except for his belief in believers' baptism. When in Edinburgh Sir William worshipped with the Glasites. In addition to believers' complete immersion, the Keiss Baptists held the 'agape' or love feast, the washing of feet and the singing of hymns. When his attempt to rebuild his residence crippled him financially the laird removed to Edinburgh, but he left the meeting in charge of his steward, John Budge, whom he had himself baptized. Sinclair died in 1768 and is buried in Canongate. In 1797 James Haldane† visited Keiss and found the Baptists did not celebrate Communion as they did not have a pastor, and that they went as far as Edinburgh for their baptisms. When he again visited in 1803 he found about 20 met in a building of turf and stone. Some 30 years later it was reported that about 60 attended services. Their first settled pastor was James Scott in 1860.

deKELDELETH, Robert. *fl. c.* 1250. Chancellor of Scotland and first mitred Abbot of Dunfermline (1240–52). He obtained permission for his monks to wear fur caps during services, except during the Elevation of the Host, a carefully guarded privilege which indicates the misery of attempting to worship in draughty, unheated buildings however impressive and beautiful. He was a clever but over-ambitious man who had to be reminded that certain privileges, equal to those of a bishop, did not extend beyond his abbey bounds. It was during his abbacy that miracles began to be recorded at the tomb of Queen Margaret†, and application was made to Rome for her beatification. Andrew Wyntoun writes in his *Orygynale Cronykil,*

'That yeir with veneratioun,
Was maid the translatioun
Of Sainct Margret the haly quene;
A fair miracle thair was sein. . . .'

To move Margaret to a shrine behind the high altar would leave her rather worldly spouse blocking the nave in assymetrical isolation and so it was fortunate that the saint's coffin refused to be lifted forward until Malcolm was carried up beside her,

'Her cors they tuik up, and bair ben,
And thaim interrit togedder then.
Swa trowit all they that gadderit thair
Quhat honour til her lord scho bair.'

In 1251 the Abbot fell under suspicion of a royal plot, resigned from his Chancellorship and Abbacy, but did not accept defeat. He quietly transferred to the Cistercian order, became a monk at Newbattle and fourteen years after leaving Dunfermline was appointed Abbot of Melrose.

KELMAN, John. *See* Drummond, Henry (1).

KELSO ABBEY (Roxburghshire). When Earl of Huntingdon, David I visited Tiron, near Chartres and brought to Scotland the Tironenses, a reform branch of Benedictines who stressed the place of craftsmanship and lay-brothers in monastic life — hence the word 'tiros' = apprentices. Four major abbeys were eventually formed, of which the parent was at Selkirk (*c.* 1113). The French monks found this an exposed and windy site, and 15 years later moved to Kelso where they built their abbey. It was frequently ravaged and burnt by the English, so badly by Hertford in Henry VIII's reign that there was little left for the Reformers to destroy. It is said that the monks themselves took arms and tried in vain to defend their property. None of the conventual buildings stand today, but there survives a substantial part of the church, which has been compared to the best Norman architecture in England and an example of the 'powerful simplicity' which characterized buildings of the order of Tiron.

opposite:
Kelso Abbey

KENNEDY, Quintin. *c.* 1520–65. Son of the Earl of Cassillis. In many ways the Scottish Erasmus, holding firmly to accepted doctrine but attacking fearlessly the corruption and worldliness of the Church. Kennedy is usually described as the last Abbot of Crossraguel† but more correctly he was its first 'Commendator'. He was never a monk but a secular priest who was given the abbey 'in commendam'. This device was often employed to secure revenue for an absentee nominal abbot, sometimes a member of the royal family, and later it was adopted as the means for secularizing the monastic lands. His uncle, William Kennedy, had held the office of Abbot before him and it was he who was Crossraguel's last Abbot. Quintin Kennedy's *Compendius Tractive* (1558) was both a defence and criticism of the old Church — '. . . what wonder is it, when such disguised personages are chosen to have Christ's flock in guiding, that the simple people be

wicked? The poor, simple people so dearly bought by the blood and death of Jesus Christ miserably perish.' He made no defence of the papal system as practised in his day nor did he fail to denounce abuses in the Church, yet he saw great dangers in abrogating its authority and doubted the ability of his 'simple men' to interpret the doctrines of the faith. A proposed debate at Ayr between Kennedy and the Reform preacher Willock did not take place because agreement could not be reached on the conditions, but it was inevitable that Knox† and he, the two best brains and principal contenders, should meet. At times they seemed near to agreement: as Knox said, 'on the verray point of a Christian agreement'. But things had gone too far and forces were moving to polarization. The climax came in 1562. Kennedy had been giving much study to his views on the mass and in his chapel at Kirkoswald he read out certain 'theses' as Luther had

done, the accepted preliminary to an argument. Knox accepted the challenge and announced that he would appear the next Sunday. Kennedy, however, drew back when he realized that Knox was to have a band of Protestant followers with him and that the debate would likely degenerate into rowdy argument. It was later arranged that a formal debate in the classical syllogistic form would take place in Maybole but this apparently completely bored the spectators on both sides who had turned up in sufficient numbers to pack the hall. The verbatim report of this three-day marathon debate was lost until a copy turned up in the famous library of Boswell at Auchinleck. In the preliminary correspondence, Kennedy pled that they should have 'familiar, formal and gentill reasoning'. Knox ostentatiously declared that he 'had come to preach Jesus Christ crucified to be the only saviour of the world'. To this came the gentle but cutting reply 'Praise be to God that was nae newings in this countrie or ye war borne'. Knox made the sour answer 'I greatlie doubt if ever Jesus Christ was truly preached by a papistical priest or monk'. It was Erasmus and Luther all over again. By the third day most spectators were leaving while Kennedy himself took ill. Knox proposed that the contest be resumed later at Ayr but this never happened and within two years Kennedy was dead.

KENNEDY, William. *See* Crossraguel; Kennedy, Quintin.

KENNETH [Cainnech] of Aghaboe. *c.* 521–99. Contemporary of Columba†, with whom he was educated in Ireland. When plague struck the community of St Mobi at Glasnevin, Dublin, Columba fled north to his native Derry and Kenneth to St Docc of Llancarfan — which might confirm the tradition that he was an Irish 'Pict' or P-speaking Celt, who would understand both the Welsh (Brythonic) and east Scottish (Pictish) tongues. His main monastery was Aghaboe (Cow Field) in Co. Laois but he seems to have travelled widely in Scotland, sometimes with Columba. Adamnan† tells of Kenneth and his party reaching Iona† just after a great storm, having followed it across the country and he also tells of the 'Saints' Mass' on Aileach

an Naoimh† or Hinba at which Kenneth was present. He seems to have penetrated to the east of Scotland and he has been called 'The Apostle of Fife'. Kennoway certainly seems connected with him and his name is remembered in Pitkinnie, Mountquhanie, Strathkinness and Ramornie. He was with Columba at the fort of King Brude at Inverness. His *Vita* has a story of his finding a woman and her child nearly dead with exposure in the Great Glen; he and his companions set a fire going and revived them both and the place was afterwards marked by a cross. There is an Inchkenneth Island near Iona where Boswell and Johnson spent a night.

KENNOWAY (Fife). *See* Kenneth.

KENTIGERN [Cynderyn: Mungo] *c.* 514–612. The only sure fact about this missionary is the date of his death in the Welsh annals. Jocelyn, monk of Furness, was commissioned (*c.* 1150) to rewrite the saint's *Life* for use in Glasgow cathedral, where a smaller *Life* (the Herbertian) had been in use. It is from these mediaeval MSS and some notes in the Aberdeen and other breviaries that the traditional story has been compiled. Thenew†, this traditional 'history' states, bore him by the shore at Culross where he was educated by the aged Serf† in his monastic school. He then moved to Glasgow where the ruler Morken opposed him and he fled to Wales where he is known as Cynderyn. He met St David, or Dewi, founded two monasteries — Llancarfan in the south and Llanelwy (St Asaph's) in the north. When the friendly King Rederech came to power in Strathclyde he returned north and laboured at Hoddom and district before finally fixing his see at Glasgow where he was visited by St Columba. As well as the Welsh contacts mentioned there are dedications to the saint in Cumbria (particularly Crosthwaite near Keswick), in Dumfries and the Lothians, in Clydesdale and in Aberdeenshire; indeed generally throughout Scotland he is widely remembered, but this may well be due to a revival of interest in his cult in the eleventh century. Jocelyn also states that he evangelized in Orkney, Iceland and Norway: surely an extravagant claim. Throughout the *Life* many miracles are ascribed to him, the best known being the recovery of a ring from a salmon. Many of these are 'standard' miracles used by the hagiographers for several saints, while others (as the salmon) have parallels in Celtic mythology. Modern critical scholarship has shown that all the mediaeval *Life* is suspect, while several incidents are obviously spurious. Professor Kenneth Jackson believed that his connection with St Serf, his meeting Columba, his Welsh and Cumbrian traditions, are all late additions to the life of a missionary whose influence did not extend far beyond the confines of Glasgow. Other scholars (Professor MacQueen) would not be quite so destructive, accepting that some of the traditional material may date back to near the time of the saint. Another view is that his mission was largely around Hoddom in Dumfriesshire. Kentigern probably means 'Lord of the Hounds' of which Mungo is most likely a colloquial version, and not (as Jocelyn thought) 'my dear one'.

KILBLANE (Bute and Renfrewshire). *See* Blane.

KILBRIDE (Lanarkshire and Wigtownshire). *See* Bride.

KILCHATTAN BAY (Bute). *See* Blane.

KILCONQUHAR (Fife). *See* Gillespie Church.

KILCURDY (Inverness-shire and Angus). *See* Curitan.

KILMACHALMAIG (Bute) and **KILMACHUMAIG** (Crinan, Argyll). *See* Colman of Dromore.

KILMANY (Fife). *See* Chalmers, Thomas.

KILNINVER (Argyll). *See* Campbell, J. McLeod.

KILPATRICK, William B. *See* Burns, William C.

KILRAVOCK (Inverness-shire). *See* Rose, Hugh.

KILSYTH. *See* Burns, William C.; Cambuslang.

KINELLAR (Aberdeenshire). *See* Restalrig.

KINGARTH (Bute). *See* Blane.

KINGOODIE (Invergowrie). *See* Curitan.

KING'S COLLEGE, ABERDEEN. *See* Elphinstone, William.

KINLOSS (Moray). *See* Reid, Robert.

KINMUCK (Aberdeenshire). This village, near Inverurie, formerly housed the largest community of Quakers in Scotland. More properly known as the Religious Society of Friends, these followers of George Fox attracted attention and consequent persecution because they so obviously differed from other Christian bodies — simple grey clothing, refusal to take an oath, use of 'thou' and 'thee', lack of form and formality in services and, especially, their refusal to retaliate when molested. The Kinmuck meeting was founded by Patrick Livingstone of Montrose, and in addition to a school and a cottage, which from 1681 housed the services until a meeting-house was added in 1716, had also the usual simple burial ground with uniform headstones, bearing only name and date, with the month indicated by a figure to avoid use of the pagan titles. The number of Friends in the area declined and the meeting ceased. The last recorded interment was in 1946.

KINNESSWOOD (Kinross-shire). *See* Bruce, Michael.

KINTORE CHURCHYARD. *See* Inverurie.

KIRK, John (1). 1832–1922. Sir John Kirk was born in Barry Manse, Angus, but most of his youth was spent at Arbirlot to which parish his father had removed. He was educated at Madras College and Edinburgh University where he was a fellow student in medicine of the future Lord Lister. On Livingstone's famous 1853–64 expedition into the heart of Africa, Kirk was his chief officer and one of the few who could stand up to Livingstone's autocratic temperament. He acted as botanist and naturalist as well as medical officer, having previously held an army medical appointment in the Crimean campaign. Although near to the heart of the missionary movement he was never ordained and later, like Livingstone, he left the movement to enter the consular service, becoming Consul-General at Zanzibar where he was instrumental in securing the abolition of the slave trade. He was knighted in 1881 and died in retirement at Sevenoaks at the age of 90.

KIRK, John (2). (E. U. minister). *See* Morison, James.

KIRKBEAN (Dumfriesshire). *See* Maxwell, Willielma.

KIRKCALDY. *See* Irving, Edward.

KIRKCUDBRIGHT. *See* Cuthbert.

KIRKGUNZEON (Stewartry of Kirkcudbright). *See* Hepburn, John; Simpson, Elspeth.

KIRKMADRINE (Wigtownshire; AM). A set of most ancient Christian burial stones beside a ruined chapel in an isolated, windswept situation. Pronunciation is important here for it has a bearing on the derivation of the name. Locals accent the last syllable, as either 'ine' or 'een', so the suggestion that the name is a corruption of Kirkmaiden cannot be correct. Sir Herbert Maxwell thought it was after Martin, but this is unlikely; Forbes took it from St Medran, but there was a Saint Dryne or Draigne, says Watson, although nothing seems to be known about him. The site is typically Celtic and seems to have been used for Christian burials from the earliest times to at least the tenth century. Preserved behind armour-plated glass in the gable of the decayed old church are three remarkable Christian stones or roughly cut pillars: (*a*) A chi-rho cross and the wording in Latin 'Here lie the holy and distinguished priests, Ides, Viventius and Mavorius'; (*b*) A similar stone with wording '. . . s and Florentius'; (*c*) A different design of cross and the inscription 'initium et finis' (the beginning and the end). Chi-rho are the Greek letters Ch (written X) and R (written P) and represent the first part of the word Christ. These lent themselves to being carved (or embroidered) in many varied forms. Gradually the 'P' became smaller and the perfect cross form was evolved. The Kirkmadrine stones, with those at Whithorn† illustrate the evolution of the cross symbol.

KIRKMAHOE (Dumfriesshire). The name probably commemorates a Celtic missionary who figured prominently in the Solway area in the fifth–sixth century. Mochaoi, pronounced 'mahee' is recorded in early Irish records as a convert of St Patrick. He set up a monastery in the island of Nendrum in Strangford Lough after driving out the pagan chief Maccuil, who landed on the Isle of Man and later was converted, becoming almost its patron saint (in Maughold parish is an ancient 'kill' and stones). There appears to have been close relations between Nendrum and Candida Casa (Whithorn). The patron saint of Wigtown may not be Machutus, as is generally claimed, but this Irish Mochaoi. He may also be commemorated at Clashmahew near Stranraer and less surely, at some other Scottish places.

KIRKOSWALD (Ayrshire). *See* Kennedy, Quintin.

KNOX, John. 1505–72. Born near Haddington. From the Grammar School there he went to Glasgow University. Priest, notary, tutor to gentlemen's sons until 1547 when he emerges as preacher of Reformation doctrines. Embroiled in the religious politics of the time, he served for a period as galley-slave, sought safety in the Protestant England of Edward VI but on the accession of Mary Tudor moved to Geneva where he took charge of the English congregation. Brought back with him to Scotland the Calvinist theology and polity and ministered in Edinburgh in the High Kirk (St Giles). His most important achievement was, with the help of his brother ministers, *The First Book of Discipline*, which formed a blueprint for the rebuilding on protestant lines of the ecclesiastical, social and educational fabric of Scotland. His life is so well known and there are so many biographies that we may better spend our space on lesser characters, but this is not to underestimate Knox, who of recent times has suffered a poor press, often in articles by those who know little of the Presbyterian tradition. Suggestions that he was a woman-hating image-basher who stamped out the native gaiety of the Scot should be examined very critically. Remember, too, that Knox used a prayer-book and accepted a type of Bishop: modern Presbyterianism is moulded more to the pattern set by Andrew Melville† than that of John Knox.

KYLE, James. *See* Gordon, Charles.

LADY YESTER'S PARISH, EDIN-BURGH. *See* Caird, John; Greyfriars.

LANG, Cosmo Gordon. *See* Tait, A. C.

LARGHILL (Stewartry of Kirkcud-bright). *See* Simpson, Elspeth.

LAUCHLISON, Margaret. *See* Wigtown.

LAUDER, Thomas. *See* Dunkeld.

LEE, Robert. 1804–68. Founder of the small but influential party in the Church of Scotland known as the Scoto-Catholics of which, a generation later, the leaders were Cooper, Wotherspoon and Sprott. He sought to recover for the Presbyterian services something of the form and dignity which they had possessed at the time of the first Reformers before they had been influenced by English Puritanism. Born at Tweedmouth, he distinguished himself in Classics at St Andrews. His first charge was to the chapel-of-ease at Arbroath, followed by a short ministry at Campsie before he was called to Old Greyfriars, Edinburgh in 1843. The following year he received his D.D. and in 1847 was appointed Professor of Biblical Criticism at Edinburgh University which in those days did not necessitate relinquishing his charge. The Disruption had just denuded the Established Church of almost all its outstanding figures and left the way open to young men like Lee for rapid promotion. He was made Dean of the Thistle and recognized as one of the leaders of the Church. In the meantime Old Greyfriars† was burnt down and for twelve years Lee and his people worshipped in the Assembly Hall which was a blessing in disguise for it enabled him to further his high-church ideas. In the restored building he had stained or painted glass, an organ (although for a time he was not allowed to use it at services) and a prayer-book compiled by him after the pattern of the early reformed liturgies. He died at Torquay and is buried in the Grange Cemetery, Edinburgh.

LEIGHTON, Robert. 1611–84. Successively minister, in Presbyterian orders, at Newbattle, Principal of Edinburgh University, reordained privately in 1661 and soon afterwards consecrated bishop in Westminster Abbey to serve first in Dunkeld, and then from 1670 for four years as Archbishop of Glasgow. He retired to spend the last ten years of his life in quiet study as an English clerical gentleman in the Sussex village of Horsted Keynes. The full details of Leighton's life are so readily available and so well-known that they need not be repeated here, except to issue a caveat against accepting him as a type or father-figure of oecumenicity and reconciliation, which is the current but too superficial interpretation of this strangely repressed personality (his father had had his ears cut off and been horribly mutilated by the high-church party in England). He is still respected but seldom read as a theologian, but it is not often remembered that S. T. Coleridge, himself one of the deepest thinkers in religious philosophy of the last century, based his own central work *Aids to Reflection* on the writings and sayings of the Archbishop.

LENNON, James. *See* Blairs College.

LEUCHARS (Fife). The parish church possesses a Romanesque apse and chancel with beautiful interior and exterior arcading and a sixteenth century bell-turret which blends wonderfully well with the older work and the modern nave. With the construction of a by-pass round the village the church reverts to something like its former serenity, although the jets from the nearby RAF air-field still shriek above it. In spite of its antiquity and beauty Leuchars church can boast little history, except for having for 30 years as minister Alexander Henderson (1583–1646) who was installed against the wishes of the parishioners and entered (the story goes) through the window for his induction. His political and ecclesiastical opinions changed and he became the intellectual force behind both the National Covenant and the Solemn League. Early in life he taught philosophy at St Andrews and for his last six years of life was rector of Edinburgh University.

LIBERTON (Edinburgh). *See* Begg, James.

LIFF (Dundee). *See* Foulis Easter.

LINDISFARNE (Holy Island, Northumbria). *See* Aidan; Cuthbert.

LINDORES ABBEY (Fife). *See* Abdie Kirk.

LINLATHEN (Angus). *See* Erskine, Thomas.

LINLITHGOW. *See* Winzet, Ninian.

LINSHART (Aberdeenshire). *See* Skinner, John.

LIVINGSTONE, David. 1813–73. The recent centenary of Livingstone's death has produced a mass of literature, some of it written apparently with the express purpose of 'debunking' yet another Victorian idol. It has, however, led more soberly to a fresh estimation of his achievements and has rightly uncovered the cracks in the hero's life-story which Victorian biographers foolishly conspired to keep secret. He was, at the best, a thoughtless husband whose lack of real concern drove Mary Moffat, daughter of his older missionary colleague Robert Moffat†, to an early death. He was incapable of working with a team and so he provoked hostility because of his unfairness to his assistants. Contrary to the usual picture of him as the devoted gospel missionary, he was much more interested in exploration, in consequence of which his relations with his parent body, the London Missionary Society, deteriorated; whenever a post in secular exploration offered, he accepted it. He had great sensitivity to, and understanding of, the African character — qualities which few of his contemporaries possessed — and he had the insatiable urge to explore and the ability to withstand intolerable hardships. His weakness in exploration seems to have been an inability ever to accept that he had been wrong, which caused much wastage of strength and many needless miles on more than one occasion. The Muslim slave-traders, who were invariably portrayed with exaggerated viciousness in Victorian biographies, were in the end those who cared for him during his last year of life. He was personally a devout Christian whose faith never wavered. His birthplace in Blantyre, with the surrounding traces of

Livingstone birthplace and memorial, Blantyre

the mills and grounds, not only provides a unique summer outing but its carefully kept museum is the best introduction to his life story. *See also* note on John Kirk.

LIVINGSTONE, Patrick. *See* Kinmuck.

LLANCARFAN. *See* Kenneth; Kentigern.

LLANELWY (St Asaph's). *See* Kentigern.

LOCH INSCH (Kingussie). *See* Adamnan.

LOCH LEVEN (Kinross-shire). *See* Serf.

LOCH MORAR. *See* Macdonald, Hugh.

LOCHNAW (Wigtownshire). *See* Agnew, Sir Andrew.

LOCH NESS. *See* Dun Dearduil.

LOGAN, John. *See* Bruce, Michael.

LOGIE AIRTH [Airthrey] (Stirling-shire). On the Sheriffmuir side-road just off the A91 stands the modern church of Logie (1805) and ruins of a very ancient building, probably dating in parts from 1380. The fact that there is no village near the church and that it is the parish church for Causewayhead a mile distant, is due to the laird's removal of the houses from within sight of his estate of Airthrey, now occupied by the new Stirling University. Robert Haldane† was once owner and it was while he was having the house rebuilt by Robert Adam and was redesigning the policies that the simple faith of one of the workmen changed him into the great evangelical benefactor who built the 'Tabernacles'. One of the Logie ministers Alexander Hume (1597–1609) was a poet of note and author of *The Day Estival*. But Logie Airth may well be much older than its old kirk. It bears all the signs of a typical Celtic site, under the shadow of a face of yellow rock known as Carlin Crag, part of the lofty Dumyat, on whose summit a small Pictish fort may still be traced, the strong-hold of the Miaetae, the most southerly Pictish tribe. Wyntoun tells that St Serf† came here and it is a much more likely place for his headquarters than Culross. It is possible there is an even earlier connec-tion, with Palladius who, we are told by Prosper of Aquitaine, was sent by the Pope 'to the Scots who believed in Christ'. Most scholars take this to refer to Ireland, home of the Scots, and point to Co. Wicklow for

the sites of the three churches he is said to have founded. The name of one was Dom-nach Airte, the Lord's High Church. One Irish scholar (Canon Meissner) has argued strongly that Palladius came to the Scots in Britain, and there were Scots here as well as in the west of Scotland. He suggested Airth, by the Forth, as the place of this lost church of Palladius. But if he did come to Scotland then Airth is a flat and unlikely site while a strong claim could be made that Logie Airth would fit. If this be so — and there is a tradition that Palladius crossed Scotland to die at Fordoun — then two early Christians may lie in this old graveyard, for it is at 'The Lord's Church of the High Field' 'where the holy men of the family of Palladius, Sylvester and Salonius are honoured'. Such comments would need to pass the critical eye of the historian, but they seem very possible when one is actually beneath the shade of these ancient walls, when, as their old minister wrote,

'The misty rocke, the clouds of rain,
From tops of mountains skaills,
Clear are the highest hills and plain,
The vapours take the vales.'

Incidentally, among the parishioners, or near neighbours, were Robert Louis Stevenson and the infamous Madeline Smith, both of whom took holidays at Bridge of Allan.

LOGIE ELPHINSTONE. *See* Inverurie.

LOTH [Leudonus]. *See* Thenew.

LOUDON (Ayrshire). *See* Macleod, Nor-man.

LUTHERMUIR (Kincardineshire). *See* Skinner, John.

MACCUIL [Maughold]. *See* Kirkmahoe.

McCULLOCH, William. *See* Cambus-lang.

MACDONALD, Donald. *See* Macfarlane, Donald.

MACDONALD, George. 1824–1905. Born in Huntly where a strong evangelical dis-senting tradition influenced his religious thought just as the local landscape and customs formed the background to much of his literary work. Up to the end of the first quarter of this present century it was his novels, especially *David Elginbrod*, which were generally appreciated but in recent years it is *Phantastes* and his children's stories which are interesting educationists and psychologists. From Aberdeen he went to the Congregational College at Highbury and from that time his contacts with Scotland were limited to vacations. He had an unfortunate ministry at Arundel where his office-bearers cut his salary in half because they disapproved of his liberal views. He moved to Manchester where he hired a room and preached to a small gathered congregation, but the numbers did not increase. He was unsuccessful in academic life for when he applied for a post in his college library he was turned down, just as later, when he competed for the Edinburgh Chair of Rhetoric it went to Masson. He was not finding it easy to get much of his work published; *David Elginbrod* was rejected by several publishers. Even when he returned to Huntly he was not asked to preach. He blamed many of his failures on popular suspicion of his liberalism, but there are people who never quite manage to reach that for which they aim, and perhaps George Macdonald was among these. He had undoubted talent, much of which is only beginning to be understood, but he surrounded himself for the most part with friends who were of giant stature and beside whom his less weighty intellect was dwarfed. Among these friends were Ruskin, who seems to have sought his advice often, Thomas Carlyle, Lady Byron, who helped him financially and in many ways, Erskine of Linlathen†, Octavia Hill, Norman MacLeod†, Professor Blackie and F. D. Maurice. He attended Maurice's church in Vere Street, London, and became a member of the Church of England. He had a very happy home life although an early lung illness kept recurring and demanded long holidays in Italy, which as his literary talents came to be recognized, he could afford. In 1897 there came upon him what his son, in his biography of his father, called 'his long vigil'. He lost almost all his faculties and endured eight years before he joined his faithful and caring wife who had died in 1902.

MACDONALD, Hugh. d. 1773. Bishop of the Highland Vicariate of the Roman Catholic Church for 42 years before his death. At the '45 Rising he strongly advised the clan chiefs against taking any part as the time was not ripe. He was returning from Edinburgh when he was told the Prince had landed and he hurried to Moidart where he was rowed out to the frigate in Loch-nam-Uamh and met him, begging him to return to France. When his warning was disregarded he blessed the Standard at Glenfinnan and appointed several priests as chaplains to the Jacobite army. 'They wore highland dress with sword and pistol and were given the rank of Captain' (P. F. Anson *Underground Catholicism in Scotland*). Later Bishop Hugh took refuge alongside Lord Lovat on an island in Loch Morar — an unwise act for he had to escape to the continent on Lovat's arrest. When he returned later he was imprisoned and sentenced to banishment. This he appears to have eluded by assuming a variety of names — Mackenzie and Scott among others. During the most difficult times he hid in the Cabrach but he managed to fulfil his episcopal duties, latterly having his nephew John Macdonald as coadjutor.

MACDOUGALL, Duncan, of Lorn. *See* Ardchattan Priory.

MACFARLANE, Alexander. *See* Macfarlane, Donald.

MACFARLANE, Donald. 1834–1926. Free Church minister at Raasay who, with the Rev. John Macdonald of Shieldaig and Mr Alexander Macfarlane, schoolmaster of Raasay, on 28 July 1893 formed the first presbytery of the Free Presbyterian Church. Many of the more conservative ministers and elders of the Free Church, especially in the Highland areas, had been increasingly uneasy about two movements gathering strength in their denomination: (*a*) Toward a union with the United Presbyterian Church, a body affirming 'Voluntary' principles, i.e. no State connection. The Free Church had always maintained that it accepted the principle of 'Establishment' and that the State had a duty to recognize and uphold the Church while leaving her free and unfettered in all religious matters — 'The Crown Rights of the Redeemer'. The 'Constitutional Party' to which Macfarlane and the Highland ministers belonged resented any union which would introduce 'New Light' views. (*b*) Allied to this was a movement to introduce a 'Declaratory Act' to weaken the strict adherence to the Westminster Confession. The U.P. Church had such an Act already (*see* Cairns, John) and it was obvious that the Free Church must have a similar one if union were to take place. In 1892 such an Act was passed and Donald Macfarlane rose to table a protest. This was not received and on the way home he preached at Kames and the congregation decided to leave the Free Church. His own did the same, a Glasgow congregation (John Knox) followed, and the secession, mainly of congregations in the Highlands and Islands, took the name Free Presbyterian. In 1900 when the Free Church united with the U.P., the majority took the name United Free, while the minority, the 'Constitutionalists' kept the title Free Church. But any idea of union between the two minorities was in vain; feelings were bitter because those who remained outside the Union in 1900 had not supported their brethren in 1892. They remain apart today but to the outsider the only visible distinction is that in the streets of Inverness the F.P. minister may be seen wearing his white tie while his Free Church counterpart (the 'Wee Free') has accepted the Roman collar. They differ slightly on some points — prayer at the graveside, church soirées, Scouts and Guides — and in their grounds of opposition to the Declaratory Acts.

McGAVIN, William. *See* Scott, Andrew.

MACKINTOSH, Charles Rennie. *See* Queen's Cross Church.

MacLEOD, John. 1872–1948. Principal of the Free Church College, Edinburgh and D.D. of Aberdeen. Born at Fort William, MacLeod was a brilliant student at Aberdeen Grammar School and University. He refused a classical scholarship to Oxford and enrolled at New College, Edinburgh for the Free Church ministry. The church was rapidly polarizing into two schools of thought — those for or against the 'New Theology' and new views on the

inspiration of scripture. MacLeod shared with many Highlanders distrust of the new ways and after one session left New College. Two years teaching at the Nicolson Institute, Stornoway, largely to improve his Gaelic, were followed by the completion of his divinity studies at the more conservative Assembly's College, Belfast. In the meantime the Free Presbyterian Church had been formed by a small group led by Donald Macfarlane†. MacLeod joined them, was licensed by the F.P. Presbytery and in 1897 ordained to Lochbroom, whence he was called, four years later, to Kames, Argyllshire. In 1900 the Free Church was again divided and the minority, retaining the title, repealed the Declaratory Act which had caused so much heartache to the Highlanders. This 'Recissory Act' made it possible for those of John MacLeod's views to rejoin and in 1905 he and three other ministers were admitted. Soon afterwards he was elected to the Chair of Greek and New Testament Exegesis in the College on the Mound. In 1913 he relinquished the post to return to the pastoral ministry in the Free North, Inverness, a charge of over 2,000 members. During his 17-year ministry he travelled extensively for his Church throughout the world and at home he was one of the most respected voices of the Highlands. In 1920 he was Moderator of the Free Church and in 1927 his university gave him the D.D. In this year also he was appointed Principal of the College but did not give up his Inverness charge. In 1930 he left Inverness to become Professor of Apologetics, Natural Science and Pastoral Theology, a position from which he retired in 1942.

MACLEOD, Norman. 1812–72. In 1843 the Church of Scotland found herself denuded of almost all her leaders and almost all her ministers; prominent among those who remained in the Establishment, although aware of her weaknesses, was Norman Macleod. He was even more aware of the dangers of secession and set himself the task of purifying and rebuilding the National Church he loved. His grandfather had been a much loved minister in Morven and his father minister in Campbeltown, where Norman was born. After charges at Loudoun and Dalkeith he became minister at the Barony, Glasgow with a parish population of 87,000. Here he followed the methods and policies of Dr Chalmers† — the Church must care for the bodies and the social welfare of her people as well as for their souls. Not only was he outstandingly successful as parish minister, but he pioneered religious journalism as editor of and writer for *Good Words*, which in those days was widely read throughout Scotland and beyond. In addition he gave much time to work for the wider church, home and foreign missions and Parliamentary lobbying for removal of the restrictions on the Established Church which had caused the Disruption. A later minister of Barony, John White (who had the charge for 40 years, 1911–51), building on the foundations which Macleod had laid by his work to re-establish the Auld Kirk in the hearts of the nation, was able to bring together most of the heirs of the 1843 crisis in the Union of 1929. Lord Macleod of Fuinary (Dr George Macleod) is Norman Macleod's nephew.

MACMILLAN, John. *See* Balmaghie Church.

McNAB, John. *See* Mylne, Andrew.

McRAE, David. *See* Gilfillan, George.

McRAE, James. *See* Barclay, John.

MADRAS COLLEGE, ST ANDREWS. *See* Kirk, John.

MAGDALEN CHAPEL, EDINBURGH. Entered from the Cowgate, with its little tower best seen from George IV Bridge which now overshadows it, this is one of the very few pre-Reformation buildings in the city. It was founded by Michael MacQueen and his wife Janet Rhynd early in the sixteenth century as a chapel and hospice for poor men, and entrusted to the care of the Guild or Incorporation of Hammermen. It was extensively used for the new or Reformed worship by the early Reformers, early General Assemblies met here and later the National Covenant was signed within its walls. It continued to function as the Chapel of the Hammermen up to 1863 and was also used for meetings of such bodies as the Bereans (*see* Barclay, John). It is now in the care of the Heriot-Watt

University. There is some good stained glass, a seemly interior with wrought iron emblems of the Hammermen, benefaction boards and an atmosphere redolent of the days of the deacons of the Edinburgh Trades.

MAIDEN STONE. *See* Inverurie.

MAITLAND, Frederick Lewis. *See* Abdie Kirk.

MALACHY [Maelmadoc]. *See* Soulseat.

MARGARET, Queen and Saint. 1045–1093. About 1070 this remarkably astute but utterly devout Anglo-Hungarian princess, friend of Archbishop Lanfranc of Canterbury and Turgot of Durham, found herself 'shipwrecked' at Rosyth within hailing distance of the eligible Scottish widower prince, Malcolm Canmore. It did not take her long to cover the nine miles to his 'Dun-ferm-linn' (tower by the crooked burn). Here she shared life with her much less saintly husband and laid plans for the replacement of the decaying 'Celtic' Church by the efficient, standardized 'Western' or 'Roman' model. Her own building, probably on the site of a still older Celtic 'cill' can still be seen under the gratings of the romanesque and gothic Abbey which was built in stages of greater and greater glory till it reached its zenith under Abbot deKeldeleth† but was already a liability when Abbot deBothwell† about 1450, had to face repairs. The Culdee monks of the Celtic Church could never have raised these pillars or sprung these arches, nor would they have been able to understand their meaning. The mediaeval clerics and craftsmen knew how to build and sing to the glory of God in their 'worthwhileship', but they in their turn were quite unable to prevent the misrule and misuse which in the end brought about their downfall, and made future Protestant generations ready to trample on the fragments of the stones. When they rebuilt the choir in the nineteenth century they unforgiveably contrived the east wall so that the blank slab where the shrine of their lady saint had stood was left outside at the mercy of the elements, remembered not at all by the majority, and by the minority, successors of the mediaeval order, only once a year at a pilgrimage and picnic.

Margaret's breviary was sold to the south and now dignifies an English university library. The present generations added a new insult when they enmeshed her cell and the stretch of the 'crooked burn' which she loved in the tar and concrete of a car-park. When the last century overlooked St Margaret it may have been in the thrill of discovering that all along they had possessed a king under the abbey floor. So they did what surely no other place in the world has dared to do; they cut in great stone letters round the tower, for all to read

KING ROBERT THE BRUCE.

Their modern successors have surely missed their opportunity; they could have capped this by adding, above or below,

ANDREW CARNEGIE THE MILLIONAIRE

or even another local who made good,

MOIRA SHEARER THE BALLET-DANCER.

No one seems to have thought of relettering the tower to read

QUEEN MARGARET OUR SAINT.

MARTYRS AND ST JOHN'S UNITED FREE CHURCH, EDINBURGH. *See* City Temple.

MATLOCK (Derbyshire). *See* Maxwell, Willielma.

MAXTON (Roxburgh). *See* Duns Scotus, John.

MAXWELL, Lady Darcy, of Pollok. *See* Ewing, Greville; Wesley, John.

MAXWELL, William, of Munches. *See* Hepburn, John.

MAXWELL, Willielma, Lady Glen-orchy. 1741–86. Lady Glenorchy, after whom two Edinburgh churches and a number of dissenting chapels in England were named, is the Scottish counterpart of the notable English evangelical gentle-woman, Selina, Countess of Huntingdon. Her father, physician at Kirkbean on the Solway, died early and she was brought up by her stepfather, Lord Alva, in Mylnes Court, Edinburgh. She married Viscount Glenorchy, heir to Lord Breadalbane, but the union was not a happy one. When she was 24 a serious illness produced a conver-sion experience to evangelical Christianity and from that time she largely withdrew from high society and surrounded herself with a small circle of high-born religious ladies and evangelical ministers. Although Taymouth Castle was the traditional home of the Glenorchy Campbells, she purchased and lived in Barnton House to be near her Edinburgh friends. The house is now demolished and the grounds are a golf-course. In 1770 she purchased St Mary's Chapel in Niddry's Wynd and opened it as an interdenominational preaching station with visiting Presbyterian and Episcopal ministers. John Wesley preached in it soon after it was opened but she was not im-pressed — 'I should have been better pleased had he preached more of Christ and less of himself.' At the time the evangelical movement in England was sharply divided into those who supported George Whitefield[†] with the Calvinist doctrine of election, and those following the Arminian Wesley[†] who stressed the freewill of man. Lady Glenorchy inclined more and more to the Calvinist position. When she was 30 her husband died and she was free to devote much of her large fortune to religious benefactions. She enabled the SSPCK to establish missionaries in the Highlands, and set about the building of a new Edinburgh chapel to replace that in Niddry's Wynd. The chapel, in the Nor' Loch valley where Waverley Station now stands, was to be part of the Established Church to which she always remained faithful, but as patroness she naturally desired a good deal of say on who was to be minister and this led to so much difficulty and frustration with the presbytery that, in poor health, she set off for England. During this and later visits she founded a number of chapels for 'Dissenters of Presbyterian or Independent views' some of which later became Congregational Churches. Ex-mouth, still a lively congregation, seems to be the only one which proudly bears her name. Others were at Buxton, Matlock Bath, where she resided for a time and, in the north, Workington and Carlisle. This last became Lowther Street Congregational Church, one of whose ministers, Thomas Woodrow, was grandfather of Woodrow Wilson, the U.S. President. One of the ministers of the Glenorchy Chapel at Matlock was father of the famous journalist and devoted Congregationalist, George Newnes who was brought up in the manse. One of her close friends, Lady Henrietta

Hope, left money which Lady Glenorchy used to erect the Hope Chapel in Bristol. After several unsuccessful attempts Lady Glenorchy got the ideal minister for her Edinburgh Chapel in Dr T. S. Jones from the Countess of Huntingdon's Connexion. He was ordained ministei of the Church of Scotland and served the chapel for 58 years. Greville Ewing† and the Bonar family were among those who owed much to the Chapel. It was demolished in 1884 to make way for the railway and because of the Disruption two chapels, Established and Free, arose. The former, in the South Side was rebuilt in this century by its minister Rev. Thomas Burns but is now removed to an extension area as Holy Trinity. Within it, in a triple coffin, rest the oft-transferred remains of the patroness. The other chapel is now also part of a union — Hillside Church. Lady Glenorchy spent her last years at the home of her niece, 15 George Square, Edinburgh.

MAYBOLE (Ayrshire). *See* Kennedy, Quintin.

MEALMAKER, George. *See* Palmer, T. F.

MEIGLE (Perthshire). The parish church possesses a remarkable mediaeval font with

Detail from Meigle font

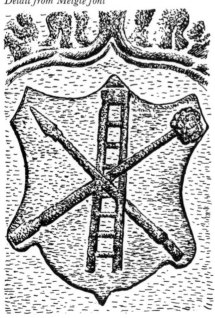

carvings of the Five Sorrowful Mysteries. The old school is now a museum (AM) of Pictish stones and crosses gathered from the churchyard and the nearby fields. Dominating the collection is an 8 ft high wheeled cross with great bosses reminiscent of the jeweller's art, and with elaborate interlacing and animal figures. The obverse has a lively panel of horsemen riding like Scythians without stirrups and in the middle a representation of Daniel in the lions' den. Perhaps because he is wearing a cassock, local legend has it that it is Queen Guinevere (local Vanora or Wener) being torn to death by hounds on Barryhill because of her infidelity with the knight Mordred. Even if King Arthur† were ever in this district the date of the cross-slab must be considerably later, so the queen must have had to wait long for her memorial, which was in the kirkyard before being brought into the museum. It is a curious fact that Vanora is still a favourite local christening name for girls. *See also* Curitan.

MELROSE. First and most glorious of the Scottish Cistercian abbeys. A Celtic community flourished at Old Melrose; it was an offshoot of Aidan's† Lindisfarne and its first Ab was one of the Anglian youths whom he had trained in the Iona tradition, Eata. Soon it nurtured Cuthbert†. This early settlement had been dead for three centuries before the 'Sair Sanct' David I founded the new Abbey in 1136 two miles up the river. Its mellow red sandstone, wealth of gargoyles and flying buttresses make it the most photographed and sung about of any Scots ruin. But it must be remembered that the present building, when it fell into decay, bore little resemblance to the original austerity and simplicity of the first Cistercian church and monastery. Here, as at the ruins of Rievaulx, it is hard to believe that Cistercians started by being puritans who despised elaboration in life and art. The remains we now see are mainly fifteenth century and later when simplicity had long since ceased to be their boast. It lay too near the Border to escape the batterings of generations of churchmen — not reformers — from the south. The real seeds of its destruction, however, lay within itself. *See* deKeldeleth, Robert.

MELVILLE, Andrew. 1545–1622. Youngest son of Richard Melville, laird of Baldovy, by Montrose, who was slain at Pinkie. He was brought up in Maryton manse, where his eldest brother was minister. The Provost of St Mary's, St Andrews, where he was sent for his studies, addressed him 'My sillie, fatherless and motherless child, it's ill to wit what God may mak' of thee yet.' To learn in detail what God made of him demands the reading of Dr McCrie's *Life of Melville*. It was a life of scholarship; teaching first at Geneva, later Principal of Glasgow University, of St Mary's College, St Andrews, Rector of the University there, and finally, in his last dreary years of exile, Professor of Divinity in the Protestant University at Sedan. He revolutionized higher education in Scotland and set a pattern of breadth in learning which only in the past century has been modified to fit English ideals of specialization. He easily takes a place among the great creative educationists of all time. His life is also a study in the struggle of the Church for freedom from the secular arm, during which Melville devised his ideal constitution for the Church in the Second Book of Discipline. He more than Knox was the founder of the Scottish Kirk as we know it in its Presbyterian form. This he did not achieve through a peaceful life in his study. Much of it was spent in exile or in suffering royal displeasure and imprisonment. In all his controversies with James VI he was encouraged and supported by his nephew, James Melville, with whom he had been brought up more as a brother in the Maryton manse. James was banished to Newcastle, Andrew to the continent and so even in exile they were separated. There is no happy ending to the Melville story; they were never reunited and both died in exile. James predeceased his uncle by eight years.

MELVILLE, James. *See* Melville, Andrew.

MENZIES, John, of Pitfodels. *See* Blairs College.

MILLER, Hugh. *See* Cromarty.

MIRREN. *See* Paisley.

MOCHAOI. *See* Kirkmahoe.

MOFFAT, Robert. 1795–1883. A more successful missionary than his celebrated son-in-law David Livingstone†. Born at Ormiston, he moved with his parents to Portsoy, to Carronshore and finally to Inverkeithing. He began at Parkhill, Polmont, as apprentice gardener, then moved to Donibristle and lastly to Cheshire at High Leigh. The journey to his new work from Inverkeithing by canal and coaster took no less than 22 days. In England he was influenced by Methodism and even more by the great missionary record of the Moravians, which captured his imagination. After several set-backs because of his lack of education, he was accepted by the London Missionary Society for training and sent to the Moravian settlement, Dukinfeld, where he assisted in the garden while he studied. Later Mary Smith, the gardener's daughter, was to follow him to Africa where they were married in St George's Church, Capetown. She had been educated at the Moravian School at Fairfield. He was 21 when he sailed for Africa and his life was spent working beyond the Orange River, largely among the Bechuana. At first there was little response and it was almost ten years before the first Christian baptisms took place, but later a strong church grew up round Kuruman where he based his headquarters. Moffat was primarily a missionary, lacking Livingstone's zeal for exploration — but also lacking any appreciation of tribal history and custom. 'Such were to him a mass of rubbish' writes his biographer. He even argued that the Bechuana had no religion at all until Christianity came. His book *Missionary Labours and Scenes* is valuable, not for insight into native life, but for the lives and conditions of the European missionaries. He overcame his lack of formal education by constant study and translated into Bechuana first St Luke's gospel and then the whole Bible. It was a pioneer but not a perfect translation, and he spent many of his later years in revision. After almost 23 years the Moffats returned to Britain on leave (1838) and in London young Livingstone, then a medical student, was much impressed when he heard Moffat lecturing. He had been hoping to go out to China but partly through Moffat's influence he changed plans and headed for Africa. He was a frequent visitor to the Moffat home at Kuruman and married the eldest daughter, Mary. In 1870, failing in health, Robert Moffat was persuaded to return to Britain to oversee his revisions through the press. His wife died soon after but he himself had 13 years to enjoy gardening at his home in Leigh, Kent.

MONIAIVE (Dumfriesshire). *See* Renwick, James.

MONCRIEFF, Alexander. 1695–1761. Heir to Culfargie estate near Abernethy, grandson of Rev. Alex. Moncrieff of Scoonie who was imprisoned and banished by Charles II, and son of Matthew Moncrieff who had succeeded his uncle as laird of Culfargie. Educated at Perth Grammar School, St Andrews and Leyden. He hesitated long about seeking ordination: 'If I be a minister I should have skill of my trade. I should thoroughly know the disease of sin and the remedy — Christ. If I know not my business I should not meddle with it.' It seems ironic that it was the very Patronage system against which he was later to rebel which put him in his parish; he, the laird, stepped into the living of Abernethy despite the warnings of his uncle, minister of Methven, who saw danger in a laird-cum-minister. When the 'Marrow' controversy was sparked off by Boston of Ettrick† he sided with the Seceders and became one of their stalwart leaders. Although their 'Associate Presbytery' declined the offer of the General Assembly to receive them back into the Established Church, they refused to quit their pulpits and the Church was unwilling to use force to eject them. For seven years Moncrieff continued in the parish church and when eventually the Assembly decided that he must be deposed he saw to it that Principal Campbell, who was to pronounce sentence, was debarred from the building. After this date (1740) he built a meeting-house and left the church and manse. Not till 1747 did the Assembly appoint a successor who discovered that Moncrieff had taken both communion plate and records. When his new chapel was opened, Moncrieff got his people to swear the 'Bond' or covenant — a practice which the Seceders adopted as an open renewal of their vows and their loyalty to the idea of a covenanted people. His services drew crowds from as far away as St Andrews. In 1742 he was appointed Professor of Divinity to the Seceding students, who met as a college or 'divinity hall' in his house for some weeks in the summer. Later he persuaded the Presbytery to set up philosophy classes. A visiting Irish bishop wrote, 'He lives in a village to the north . . . and had formed a sort of university for educating young men for their congregations . . . there were about 20 boarded there'. In the '45 he violently opposed the Jacobite army which was encamped at Perth. He divided from the more moderate Erskines over the Burgess Oath — an affirmation of loyalty certain councils imposed after the Rising which contained a clause approving the Protestant religion laid down by law. Most Seceders were content to leave the interpretation of this to individual conscience, but the 'Anti-burghers', led by Moncrieff and Gib of Edinburgh, insisted on rejection of the oath and formed a separate denomination, 'The General Associate Presbytery'. He survived longest of the four original Seceders. It was said that when he was preaching powerfully he would often pause for a long minute and his congregation would whisper 'Culfargie's awa' tae heaven.' At length he was, and his body lies in Abernethy kirkyard.

MONTGOMERY, James. *See* Caldwell, John.

MOODIE, Dwight. *See* Drummond, Henry (1).

MORAVIAN MEETING HOUSE, AYR. *See* Caldwell, John.

MORISON, James. 1816–93. Licensed by the Secession in 1839, after preaching for a short time in the Cabrach he accepted a call to Clerk's Lane, Kilmarnock. His brethren showed their disapproval of his theology by refusing to proceed with the ordination until he renounced his pamphlet *What must I do to be saved?* He drew large crowds to his services, preaching a modified Calvinism tending to Arminianism. Within a year he was libelled and tried by his presbytery and deposed by the Secession

Synod as holding 'Universal Atonement'. The only dissentient was his father, Robert Morison, who was himself deposed within a year. In 1843 four ministers, led by Morison, met in Clerk's Lane vestry and founded the Evangelical Union, with an Independent or Congregationalist polity ('. . . every church we conceive to be complete in itself — a separate church of Christ'), and with a doctrinal statement stressing universal atonement and the universality and moral nature of the Holy Spirit. It rejected any formal credal subscription, and although originally it thought of itself not as a new church but rather as a 'union' of similarly minded Christians, it quickly developed into a denomination 'as clearly marked off from other Christian Churches as any in the land' (Escott, *History of Scottish Congregationalism*). Among its early adherents was John Kirk, who had led the anti-Calvinist party in the Congregational Union and who had greatly influenced Morison's thinking. Nine Congregational Churches and four from the Secession formed the first E.U. units but by the time of its union with the C.U. it had 90 congregations. It was noted for its advocacy of total-abstinence; Brighton Street Chapel under John Kirk was the first church to use non-fermented wine for the Sacrament. Morison moved to Dundas Street Church, Glasgow, where he ministered 1851–84; he acted as tutor to the denominational seminary and received both an American and a Glasgow D.D. Shortly before his death the U.P. Synod removed the ban it had imposed on his preaching 50 years earlier. The E.U. churches united with the Congregationalists (C.U.) in 1896, bringing to the union a pioneer tradition in hymnology, a worthy record of scholarship and a liberality of Christian thought. It is even now sometimes possible to distinguish E.U. from C.U. churches as the former tended to have elders and use the *Church Hymnary* while the latter had deacons and sang from the *Congregational Hymnary* or *Congregational Praise*.

MORISON, Robert (1). 1620–83. Born and educated in Aberdeen, intended for the ministry but abandoned the thought in order to serve against the Covenanting armies. Wounded at the battle of the Brig of Dee and fled to Paris where he studied botany and zoology, and later anatomy and medicine. About 1650 became physician to the Duke of Orleans and cared for his physick garden. Appointed Professor of Botany at Oxford.

MORISON, Robert (2). *See* Morison, James.

MORKEN. *See* Kentigern.

MORRISON, Robert. *See* Burns, W. C.

MOUNTQUHANIE (Fife). *See* Kenneth.

MOUSWALD (Dumfriesshire). *See* Ruthwell Cross.

MUNGO. *See* Kentigern.

MUTHILL (Perthshire). *See* Barclay, John; Innes, Andrew.

MYLNE, Andrew. 1776–1856. Parish minister of Dollar, Founder, Chairman of Governors and Headmaster of the school which was to become world-famous. Crauford Tait, laird of Harviestoun and patron of the parish of Dollar, planned that the considerable legacy from the will of John McNab, a local lad who had run away to sea to amass a fortune, should not be spent on almshouses as the aged minister, John Watson, had intended, but that it should be used for education. He patiently prepared a likely young minister who was already spoken of highly in the educational world, so that when the charge fell vacant he might present him. Such a man he had found in Andrew Mylne, born and educated in Haddington, to which he returned as a teacher after taking his degree in Edinburgh and becoming a probationer of the Church of Scotland. He was in charge of a successful school in the capital when, in 1815, he became minister of Dollar. Within three years legal disputes over the bequest were settled and he had some £90,000 in his own hands and those of his small kirk-session. He immediately applied himself to something more than a local school — a great 'Institution' later called 'Academy' — where boys and girls together, from poor children of the parish to boarders whose parents might be abroad, would be educated in a worthy Playfair building, with beside it an avenue of teachers' houses with whom the boarders might lodge. As parish minister he was *ex officio* Chairman of Governors and had himself elected Headmaster or Rector. There was in existence a letter Mylne as minister wrote to Mylne as chairman who passed it to Mylne as rector. Perhaps naturally he was not remembered for his zeal as preacher or pastor but all his educational commitments were carried out with talent and initiative, if with no nonsense about democracy. The old school which was used before the Academy was built still stands beside the bridge over the burn which Mylne had made to shorten his journey from church to school. The church he knew is a ruin, but a perpetual lamp in the present parish church commemorates him and his manse still houses the minister. The Playfair building was badly damaged by fire in 1961; the great oil-portrait of Mylne, fierce and cross-eyed, peeled and dripped to a meaningless mass of colours as the magnificent library blazed. Modern technology was, fortunately, able to save the shell of the building and restore the interior.

MYLNE, Robert. *See* Inverary Parish Church.

NECHTAN macDERILE. *See* Curitan; Restalrig.

NECHTANSMERE (Dunnichen, Angus). *See* Restenneth.

NENDRUM (Co. Down). *See* Kirkmahoe.

NEWBATTLE (Midlothian). *See* deKeldeleth, Robert; Leighton, Robert.

NEWINGTON FREE CHURCH, EDINBURGH. *See* Begg, James.

NEW LUCE (Wigtownshire). *See* Peden, Alexander.

NEWNES, George. *See* Maxwell, Williel-ma.

NICOLSON INSTITUTE (Stornoway, Isle of Lewis). *See* MacLeod, John.

NICOLSON SQUARE METHODIST CHAPEL, EDINBURGH. *See* Ward, Valentine.

NINIAN [Nyniau]. Fifth century. Most of what pass for biographical details of this saint are conjectures now discredited by scholars. The traditional view was that he was a Briton who, about the time the Roman armies were withdrawing from Britain, went to Rome, was ordained by the Pope for work in his native land and on his return spent some time with St Martin of Tours whose missionary methods he adopted when in 497 he built the White Hut (Ad Candidam Casam) at Whithorn. He then evangelized the Picts; one version of the tradition then asserts that he was buried at Whithorn, but another connects him with the Irish Monenna and suggests he spent his last years in Ireland. The traditional picture is adapted from Bede with embellishments from a mediaeval 'Vita' by St Aelred. A much later discovery of a MS, the 'Miracula Niniani', as old as Bede, first threw doubts on the accepted story and as one 'fact' after another was questioned Ninian became more and more shadowy with no reliable dating and no secure locus. Bede's key sentence translates as:

'The southern Picts who dwell on this side of these mountains had, it is said, long before [the time of Columba] forsaken the error of idolatry and received the true faith under the teaching of Nynias . . . a most holy man of the Britons . . . his episcopal see, distinguished by the name of St Martin is now possessed by the Angles. This place is commonly called "At the White Hut".'

Difficulties are (*a*) There were no Picts in Galloway; southern Picts were those south of the 'Mounth', in roughly modern Angus, Mearns and district. Why did Ninian, a Briton with his HQ at Whithorn go to a different folk so far away to evangelize? (b) Although there are many place-names suggesting a Ninianic connection (St Ninian's, St Ringan's, St Trinnian's) they are from later language roots and may date from a time when his cult as a saint became popular. Dr W. D. Simpson traced Ninian's supposed journeys along the lines of the Roman roads and stressed that the saint was very much a Roman-British Christian. Later, however, Simpson had to discard many of the places supposedly Ninianic, e.g. St Ninian's Isle, Shetland, where early Christian treasure was unearthed beneath the floor of a chapel. Dr Ralegh Radford excavated some ancient coffins at Whithorn† and found white plastering on the lowest courses of deeply buried buildings — might this be the original Candida Casa? Scholars continued to doubt and Dr Norah Chadwick suggested that perhaps Ninian had worked among the Picts north of the Tay but from some settlement in central Scotland which had only been connected with Whithorn much later. We are not even certain of 'Ninian's' real name as we only have the Celtic in its ablative form. There was, however, an active Christian settlement around the Solway about the time of the Roman withdrawal, as Charles Thomas's excavations at Ardwall Isle† indicate.

NORTH COLLEGE STREET CHAPEL, EDINBURGH. See Aikman, John.

OGILVIE, John. 1580–1615. Born near Keith, son of the laird of Dunn, he was sent to the continent for his education, became Roman Catholic, joined the Society of Jesus and was ordained priest in 1608. The Jesuit order had been founded by Ignatius Loyola to lead the Counter-Reformation movement, particularly in those countries which had deserted 'the old faith'. This was extremely dangerous work, to be carried out in secret, with terrible penalties for detection. Fr John Ogilvie with two colleagues was ordered to Scotland, where he landed disguised as a soldier. In Edinburgh he was secretly guest of the advocate William Sinclair and in March 1614 he went south to London; it was later hinted that he had there been implicated in a plot against the king. He visited his superior in Paris and was ordered back to Scotland

where he again stayed with Sinclair for some time. On October 4 the same year he was arrested in Glasgow by order of Archbishop Spottiswoode†. Attempt at disguise was futile for it was discovered that he was carrying a portable altar, chalice, saints' relics and some incriminating correspondence. He was examined in Edinburgh and tortured until forced to reveal certain accomplices, but he steadfastly refused to recant and accept the Oath of Supremacy and Allegiance. After further severe torture he was removed to Glasgow for trial. The usual procedure was adopted to avoid the suggestion of religious persecution — the charge was not of saying mass but of refusing the authority of the king. Pressure on him to recant was rejected and he died by hanging in 1615. He was Beatified in 1929 and is remembered on March 10 — the only Scots Catholic martyr of the Counter-Reformation.

OLD ST PAUL'S EPISCOPAL CHURCH, EDINBURGH. See Ramsay, Edward.

ORMISTON (East Lothian). See Moffat, Robert.

ORONSAY, Isle of (Argyll). There is no historical support for the tradition that Columba landed on this island but did not remain because he could still see Ireland. He must, however, have known Oronsay well, and its larger neighbour Colonsay, for they are on the direct route to Ireland and to the Argyll mainland from Iona†. It is possible that there was a Celtic community here and some scholars would prefer this as Hinba rather than Aileach an Naoimh†. There are several ruins of mediaeval date, the most important being the Priory (c. 1380) with its high altar still in situ, a most attractive cloister garth and a great high cross attributed to a Prior Colin. This cross may be as late as the sixteenth century but it represents a transition from the wheeled Celtic type to the Roman crucifix and resembles the similar cross at Kilmory. Even in this remote place the stones of the Priory have been filched to build the neighbouring farm. *Drawing of Priory, overleaf.*

ORPHAN HOMES OF SCOTLAND (Bridge of Weir, Renfrewshire). See Quarrier, William.

The Cloisters, Oronsay Priory

ORR, Norman F. *See* Caldwell, John.

OSWALD. *See* Aidan.

OSWESTRY (Salop). *See* Aidan.

OSWY. *See* Aidan.

OXNAM (Roxburghshire). *See* Gillespie Church.

PAISLEY. The patron saint Mirren crossed from Bangor in Ulster where he had been head of the largest of Celtic communities. Traditionally he is linked with St Constantine† of Govan. The Abbey, originally a Cluniac priory was founded by the Norman, William Fitz Alan, in the reign of David I; he was Hereditary High Steward and the first of the Stewart line, so the Abbey benefited later from its royal connection. Cluniac monks were a branch of the Benedictines formed at Cluny in France in 910. They were known as patrons of the arts and stressed elaborate and dignified services more than manual or field work, even more than personal prayer. They adapted the original Benedictine rule but retained the black habit. There were only two such foundations in Scotland, the other being Crossraguel†. Paisley Abbey has been much restored although there is still fourteenth and fifteenth century work.

Macgregor Chalmers and Robert Lorimer were among the restorers of the fabric and there are stained glass windows including some by Burne-Jones and Strachan. Equally worth seeing in Paisley is Coats Memorial Church, the 'Baptist Cathedral', one of the many benefactions resulting from the local cotton-thread industry being in the hands of a Christian family. The church was designed in 1894 by Hippolyte Blanc in red sandstone with tower and crown steeple. A. L. Drummond writes in appreciation of it as Blanc's greatest work and adds, 'It is a reminder that the ambition to build inspiring sanctuaries was not confined to the Church of Scotland.' (*Church Architecture of Protestantism.*) It adopted a liturgical form of service unfamiliar to most Baptists.

PALLADIUS. *See* Logie Airth.

PALMER, Thomas Fyshe. 1747–1808. Although classed among pioneers of Scottish Unitarians, Palmer was born in Bedfordshire, educated at Eton and Cambridge (B.A., M.A., B.D.) and ordained to the Anglican ministry. He became a Fellow of Queen's College but when he adopted Unitarian principles he had to relinquish a brilliant academic career and leave his church. His private means were sufficient to allow him to offer his services voluntarily to William Christie of Montrose who was at the time developing the first Unitarian societies in Scotland. After assisting Christie for two years Palmer became the first Unitarian minister in Dundee (1785), a cause which died out until revived by Henry Williamson in the middle of the nineteenth century. Palmer preached widely in Scotland and in 1789 took temporary charge of the meeting at Newcastle upon Tyne. He still made his home in Dundee and it was through an incident here that he was transported to Botany Bay and had his name inscribed on the great obelisk in the Calton Burying Ground, Edinburgh, as one of Scotland's political martyrs. 'The Friends of Liberty' in Dundee was founded to further liberal and revolutionary aims, one of many such societies which followed the French Revolution and terrified the reactionary British government. Palmer lodged near the group's meeting place in the Overgate and joined almost casually after hearing a paper read by a weaver, George Mealmaker. He tidied up the grammar and, very foolishly as it turned out, undertook its publication

Thomas Fyshe Palmer

through the press and payment of the expenses. At the time the government were seeking to make an example of the 'intellectuals' who were encouraging the workers in revolution and Palmer was an obvious target. The trial at Perth under Lord Braxfield has become a classic for its politically weighted verdict. It was accepted that not only was Palmer not author of the pamphlet but had originally advised against publication, but he was sentenced to transportation. Because of his cultured background every effort was made to break his spirit; he was held in Perth prison and in the Woolwich hulks for many months before sailing under a sadistic captain. Robert Burns writes of 'the injustice done to a Unitarian minister', and Palmer is even credited with being the inspiration for *Scots Wha Hae*. With great devotion one Ellis, a Dundee weaver, accompanied him as a free emigrant and also beside him was a medical student called Boston. Mealmaker was also transported but soon got into trouble and was jailed for inciting rebellion. At Botany Bay Palmer was better treated and became an ideal 'colonial', but a strange change had come over him, obviously as a result of his traumatic experiences. He interested himself no further either in religion or politics but passed his seven-year sentence in purely commercial and materialistic enterprises. He ran a small farm, retailed rum at a large profit and later with Ellis and Boston formed a trading company for coal and seal-skins. At the end of his sentence he decided to return to Britain and bought a second-hand ship, intending to trade on the way home. Seamanship was poor and the boat was rotten and it finally grounded at the island of Guam. Palmer died and was buried there but, for some reason never explained, orders came from the U.S.A. that the body should be exhumed and taken to Boston. There is no record of what eventually happened to it.

PANBRIDE (Angus). *See* Bride; Trail, Ann Agnes.

PAPA WESTRAY (Orkney). *See* Restalrig.

PARK CHURCH, GLASGOW. *See* Caird, John.

PATRICK. *fl. c.* 440. No one doubts that March 17 is Patrick's day but scholars differ greatly about his dates. It is safer to call him 'Patrick the Briton' for the traditional Patrick story may be an amalgam of at least two saints. Many incidents in the life of Palladius (*see* Logie Airth) are suspiciously like duplications from Patrick or vice versa. The claim that he was born at Dumbarton rests on no sure evidence but on a comparatively late gloss in a MS. There is certainly a farm called Succoth near Dumbarton and Patrick's British name was Sucat, and there are, not far away, Old and New Kilpatrick, but the more likely place for his birth is Cumberland. The whole Patrician question is involved and uncertain, but the two documents he left, the *Confessio* and the *Letter to Coroticus*, are living evangelical outbursts as if from some General Booth of the Dark Ages — which is perhaps just what Patrick was. Patrick the Briton is best considered in relation to the Solway Mission of the fifth century.

PAULINUS. *See* Aidan.

PECHTHELM. *See* Whithorn.

PEDEN, Alexander. *c.* 1626–84. Born Auchincloich, near Sorn, Ayrshire, of small landowning stock, this wandering prophet of the Covenanters was no illiterate peasant; he was educated at Glasgow University, became schoolmaster at Tarbolton and was ordained minister at New Luce. After the Restoration in 1663 he was evicted and spent the rest of his life preaching on the moors and avoiding capture by the dragoons. He treated as his parish the whole south-west of Scotland and the counties of Antrim and Down. He joined the Pentland Rising and although he left the rebels before Rullion Green he was 'proscribed'. Captured at a conventicle at Knockdow, near Ballantrae, he was imprisoned on the Bass Rock for four years, with a further year in Edinburgh Tolbooth. He was sentenced to be banished but released in London. There was always some tension between Prophet Peden and the Society Men, or Cameronians, the reason for which is not now easy to uncover. On his deathbed he was visited by their young leader Renwick†.

PENDA. *See* Aidan.

PEN FOLK OF PAISLEY. *See* Balchrystie.

PETERCULTER (Aberdeenshire). *See* Curitan.

PHYSGILL (Wigtownshire). *See* Whithorn, Isle of.

PITGOBER (Clackmannanshire). *See* Foret, Thomas.

PITKINNIE (Fife). *See* Kenneth.

PITLUMBERTIE (Fife). *See* Bride.

PLUSCARDEN ABBEY (Moray). To be correct, the accent is on the first syllable only. Here in a fertile vale, well sign-posted on a side road south-west of Elgin, is an Abbey which really *is* an Abbey and not a mass of ruined stone. It was founded by King Alexander II in 1230 as a Valliscaulian priory along with Beauly† and Ardchattan† — the only examples of this order in Britain. It had the honour of being ravaged by Edward I and burned by the Wolf of Badenoch. In 1453, when the popular ardour to adopt monastic life or to donate toward it had largely passed, its strength had fallen to six monks and it changed its Order so that it might unite with the Benedictine foundation at Urquhart which had only two inmates. The last Prior, Alexander Dunbar, alienated both funds and land to his own family. The usual pattern of ruin followed and in 1943 its owner, Lord Colum Crichton-Stuart, decided to offer it to the Ministry of Works as an Ancient Monument. He had over some years offered it to various monastic communities but none had been able to face the cost of restoration. He made one last offer, this time to the Benedictine community at Prinknash and it was accepted. They would rebuild themselves; in 1948 six monks occupied the building. Since then the task has proceeded as rapidly as funds and monk-power would permit. It now has no longer the feel and appearance of a ruin but the active sanctity of a place where men pray and live. There is some excellent restoration, two delightful and meaningful chapels and some very good modern glass, particularly the window representing the Woman Clothed with the Sun from Revelation 12.

POLWARTH (Berwickshire). *See* Baillie, Lady Grisell (1).

PORTMAHOMACK (Ross-shire). *See* Colman of Dromore.

PORTOBELLO, EDINBURGH (TOWER STREET). *See* Cromarty.

PRIMMER, Jacob. 1842–1914. Born beside Leith Shore in humble circumstances, Primmer made the best use of his schooling, became a compositor, studied in the little spare time he had and at the age of 23 entered Edinburgh University to study divinity. He served in Church of Scotland mission stations at Westray, Gardenstown and (from 1876) the chapel-of-ease at Townhill, Dunfermline, then a mining village, now a suburb of the town. He never became a parish minister but remained at Townhill till his death. He was a devoted disciple of John Hope† although the suggestion that Hope financed him through college and paid for his anti-Romanist activities is incorrect. Primmer adopted an extreme low church position,

refusing the title of 'Reverend' and calling himself 'Pastor', objecting to gown and bands or to repetition of the Lord's Prayer in services. He instituted a nationwide series of so-called 'conventicles' which were deliberately framed to secure Roman Catholic opposition, and for a time he led a 'Hallelujah Army' on Salvation Army lines. Up and down Scotland he spoke from a wagon which he had secured by chains and wedges as the 'papists' delighted in pushing it down any available hill. The more the police were called in to protect him the better pleased he was. He gloried in the stones and dirt thrown at him although on some occasions he was badly hurt; at one time or another he had been chased through most Scottish towns. He had sincerity and a strange kind of bravery, as when in Dublin he stood his ground while the Hussars charged the crowd with drawn swords. He maintained that if you remained in your place they would charge round you, and fortunately for him the theory seemed to be true. At the same time Primmer carried on a long series of fierce

Pluscarden Abbey

controversies with his brother ministers in the Church of Scotland. It was a period when churches were being 'modernized' with side pulpits, lecterns and symbolic carvings, all of which were to him anathema and 'papish'. In St Giles he rose to protest at the 'liturgy' and at St Cuthbert's to protest at the font and reredos. He singled out the 'Scoto-Catholic' or high church leaders for his special displeasure and conducted a 'sanctimonious hypocrite' case against Principal Story, while he called Dr Cooper 'more like a monk than a minister'. For most Assemblies he had a protest ready and as he had a good grasp of law, quick repartee and smart humour his opponents seldom got the better of him. His greatest success in restraining the high church party was in the Barnhill case, where in the new chapel-of-ease from Monifieth the minister, Rev. T. N. Adamson, had been conducting the Sacrament with his back to the people who had to kneel at the 'altar rail' for their communion while the Holy Table was adorned with lighted candles. Largely as a result of the agitation stirred up by Primmer the minister had to give a pledge to the General Assembly of 1903 that the services would be conducted in accordance with the custom of the Church. Although Primmer differed so widely from his fellow ministers never once did he think of leaving the Established Church, and his story is in reality a tribute to the breadth and Christian understanding of that body; to the last his bitterest opponents in controversy continued to shake him by the hand. He was never, as he knew, in the slightest danger of being 'unfrocked' as he undoubtedly would have been had he proved equally difficult in the courts of the U.P. or the Free.

QUARRIER, William. 1829–1903. Born at Greenock. His father, a ship's carpenter, died of cholera in Quebec. His mother, struggling with poverty, moved to the Gorbals where she sewed for warehouses. William's first job was putting heads on pins at a shilling for a 72-hour week. Next, as apprentice shoemaker, he advanced so rapidly that at 23 he was in business on his own and eventually he owned a chain of shoe shops. He appears to have had little

contact with religion until a friend of his mother invited them both to accompany her to church. 'I was led,' Quarrier writes, 'to accept Christ as all my salvation.' He was then 17 and his enthusiasm was so great that soon he had several pews filled with his companions each week. For a time he considered entering the ministry but, probably wisely, he dismissed this idea in order to devote both his wealth and his labour to Christian social work, and in this his simple faith that God would provide was linked to his great organizational powers. In the Industrial Brigade Home, Trongate, Glasgow, he organized activities for shoe-blacks, newsboys and others which were remarkably like a modern youth club. In 1871 he opened his first orphan-home for boys in Renfrew Lane and followed it with one for girls in Renfield Street. Apart from initial advertisements for help he resolved to appoint no collectors and make no appeals, and all gifts were treated as anonymous. He moved his homes to Govan and in 1878 conceived the great plan which became The Orphan Homes of Scotland at Bridge of Weir. A central building and three cottages were the nucleus of what was to develop into a great organization retaining the form of separate units under houseparents — which his genius had recognized was the best way to retain Christian concern and love in institutional life. Eventually Quarrier gave up his business interests to devote himself entirely to this work. Later he also opened the first Scottish sanatorium (1896) and an epileptic hospital.

QUEEN'S CROSS CHURCH, GLASGOW. The only ecclesiastical building designed by the Glasgow architect Charles Rennie Mackintosh and surely one of the few attempts to employ 'art nouveau' to the glory of God. Partially despoiled in its interior some years ago — without protest from either city or presbytery — it is now threatened by new roads and motorways. Completed in 1899, it was ahead of its time and has been described as one of the outstanding church designs of the present century; with lots of dark wood inside and a queer stumpy tower outside, it is a delight to preach or worship in. The design for the tower, it has now been established, came from Merriot Church, Somerset. Mackintosh himself was not a religious man. Dispirited by his non-acceptance in his native country he retired to London, gave up architecture and turned to painting but died early in poverty and was buried in an unmarked grave.

de QUINCEY, Thomas. *See* Gilfillan, G.; Robertson, Wm. B.

RAASAY, Isle of. *See* Macfarlane, Donald.

RAINY, Robert. 1826–1906. Entered New College, Edinburgh, the year after the Disruption. He held charges at Huntly and the Free High, Edinburgh, now the library of New College. Appointed Professor of Church History at New College at the age of 36, he became Principal in 1874. While Mr Gladstone called Rainy 'unquestionably the greatest of living Scotsmen', history has been more severe in its judgement. When Professor Robertson Smith† was charged with heresy because he accepted the inevitable advance in Biblical Criticism, Rainy spoke advocating his deposition, although it was suspected that he held similar views himself and was sacrificing Smith to appease conservative opinion. He forsook the original Free Church position when his 'Voluntaryism' led him to campaign for the disestablishment of the Church of Scotland. The 'Voluntary' movement, consisting of the New Lights of the Seceders, believed in the complete separation of Church from State on the lines of the English Free Churches. Rainy's support of a political campaign for Disestablishment in Scotland led naturally to the charge that in malice he was trying to weaken the main opposing church to his own. He was, however, a talented ecclesiastical statesman to whom was largely due the union, in 1900 of the Free and the United Presbyterian Churches. One of the principal halls of New College, now used as a refectory, bears his name.

RAMORNIE (Fife). *See* Kenneth.

RAMSAY, Edward. 1793–1872. His father was sheriff of Kincardine but he himself spent most of his childhood on his uncle's Yorkshire estates and attended the Cathedral Grammar School at Durham.

From Cambridge University he went to a curacy in Somerset, then in 1824 to St George's Episcopal Chapel, Edinburgh. He moved to Old St Paul's and then in 1827 became assistant to Bishop Sandford at St John's, Princes Street. In 1830 he became rector, a post he held until his death, declining, it was said, three bishoprics. In 1846 he became Dean of the diocese, a position roughly equivalent to that of archdeacon in England. His main literary work was his *Reminiscences*, one of the classics of Scottish domestic life. Ramsay was a 'broad churchman', suspicious of the High Church movement in the Scottish Episcopal Church. He maintained an understanding of and a friendship with, the established Presbyterianism which was anathema to many of his brethren. The majority of the Anglo-Catholic or High Church party were supporters of the Scottish Prayer Book which permitted a more 'Catholic' interpretation of the service of Holy Communion than the English Book of Common Prayer. Ramsay insisted on the latter being used and so incurred the charge of Anglicizing the Scottish Church. One of his aims was to bring the two sister Episcopal churches on either side of the Border nearer together and for this, he would have pleaded, one common service was essential. He is commemorated by a Celtic cross at the west end of Princes Street, Edinburgh, close to St John's Episcopal Church.

RATHVEN (Banffshire). *See* Hay, George.

RATTRAY, William. *See* Stobhall.

REDERICH of Strathclyde. *See* Kentigern.

REGENT'S SQUARE CHURCH, LONDON. *See* Irving, Edward.

REGULUS. *See* Rule.

REID, Robert. d. 1558. Abbot of Kinloss, Bishop of the Orkneys, Prior of Beauly† — an example of the pluralism which was accepted at the time and which was among the causes of the Reformation. Born near Kinneddar, educated at St Andrews, he was appointed to Kinloss in 1526. Although in most places the impetus had largely passed from the monastic movement, Abbot Robert was still rebuilding and beautifying parts of his Abbey up to 1540 when the nave was rebuilt. Within a generation his work was all to be undone and the building already falling into ruin. He was a man of diverse interests, bringing the painter Bairhum to design altarpieces and a gardener from France to introduce fruit-trees into the district. In some ways Abbot Robert may be considered the founder of Edinburgh University as he gifted the original parcel of land for a college. The Italian scholar Ferrarius, whom Reid brought to the Abbey to teach the monks Humane Letters, left a glowing account of all that he found there. Besides his ecclesiastical dignities, Reid was a Senator of the College of Justice, and in his last ten years held office as Lord President. He died on his way home from the wedding of the young Queen of Scots to the Dauphin of France, perhaps as the result of poison administered at the behest of Catherine de Medici, whose designs on Scotland's sovereignty he had resisted.

REID, Walter. *See* Beauly Priory.

RENWICK, James. 1662–88. Son of a weaver in Moniaive, Dumfriesshire, he graduated at Edinburgh. Witnessing the public execution of Donald Cargill at Edinburgh Mercat Cross when he was 19 had a profound effect on him. He joined the United Societies, or Hillmen, who from their slender resources sent him to study in Holland, where he was ordained at the age of 21. For his first sermon at Cambusnethan he took the same text (Isaiah 26: 20) that had been the substance of Cargill's last sermon, thereby indicating that he accepted the mantle of preacher to the extreme Covenanters, those who had placed themselves beyond the scope of any toleration or pardon. He had a ministry of less than four years, all spent under the cloud of persecution. He moved through all the southwest counties and at times was still daring to hold conventicles when even Peden† considered it folly to gather people into the open. In 1684 an edict of the Privy Council forbade anyone to hold communication or association with him, but in the following year he repeated the provocative action of Richard Cameron five years earlier, by riding into Sanquhar to affix his protest at the accession of the Catholic Duke of York

as James VII. With the help of Alexander Shields he issued *An Informatory Vindication of a poor, wasted, misrepresented remnant of the suffering, anti-popish, anti-prelatic, anti-erastian, anti-sectarian, true Presbyterian Church of Christ in Scotland*. This apologia for the Cameronian's position was penned at Freminion, a lonely farmhouse half-way between Sanquhar and Muirkirk. After a narrow escape at Peebles, Renwick was taken while staying with a friend on Castlehill, Edinburgh. 'What? Is that boy that Mister Renwick whom the nation has been so troubled with?' asked the captain of the guard. The articles of the Privy Council upon which he was condemned, and the guilt of which he accepted, were all political rather than religious — that he refused the king's authority, refused to pay taxes and that he advised his followers to come armed to his meetings. The Council were reluctant to incur the odium of a new victim when events were moving toward a rebellion, and they granted a week for reconsideration. On his refusal to alter his stand it was obvious that the extreme penalty had to be exacted. This last official victim of 'The Killing Times' was executed on 17 February 1688.

RESTALRIG PARISH CHURCH, EDINBURGH. Records of the church date back to the twelfth century but its connection with the Celtic saint Triduana make an earlier foundation probable. The church was rebuilt in 1487 and its balm-well, dedicated to Triduana (whose burial place was supposedly in the church) became a major place of pilgrimage for those with afflictions of the eye. This superstition caused it to be the first target of the Reformers, who in the General Assembly of 1560 directed that 'the kirk of Restalrig as a monument of idolatrie be raysit and utterlie castin downe and destroyed'. Thereafter the Restalrig worshippers joined the Leith people in the Kirkgate Chapel which later became South Leith Parish Church. Little of the fabric remained except some portions of the choir and in 1836 these were restored and built into the present church. In 1907 the adjoining chapel of St Triduana was restored and its original well revealed. Triduana's life is admixed with the miraculous and she

Restalrig Church as it was in 1817

shares with the Galloway saint Modwenna and other female figures what might be termed the 'thorn myth'. In this the saint is the recipient of the unwelcome attentions of a princely lover, to avoid whom she pierces her own eyes and devotes herself to a cloistered life. In the mediaeval expanded legend, or tradition, of Triduana, she came north as a follower of St Curitan† with Crescentia as companion; Nactanus (obviously King Nechtan macDerile) fell in love with her at Rescobie near Forfar and she fled to Dunfallandy whence she sent him her eyes skewered on a thorn stick. After this, in one version she travelled north where she is remembered in various place-names (Kinellar, St Tredwell's in Papa Westray), in another she returned south to Restalrig to devote herself to healing and charitable works. *See also* Thenew.

RESTENNETH PRIORY (Angus; AM). This unobtrusive and little-known monastic ruin is one of the most ancient Scottish churches. It was founded soon after 710 by St Bonifacius or Curitan† at the instance of King Nechtan macDerile of the Picts. The lower courses of the stone tower are of this period. The Celtic name was EGGLES-

PETHER, St Peter's Church. Curitan was introducing Roman usages to the people north of the Tay and replacing simple names of sites after their founders by dedications to St Peter as chief of the apostles. Half a century before the foundation the battle of Nechtansmere (Dunnichen) was fought nearby when the Picts defeated the Anglians and slew their king. Alexander I had the Iona records removed here for safety. Later it appears as a small priory of

Restenneth Priory

Augustinian canons (*see* Inchmahome) and about 1160 it was placed under Jedburgh Abbey. At its prime it seems to have housed no more than six monks and by 1501 it had fallen to two. In the Wars of Independence it was sacked and burnt by the English. It fell into ruin after the Reformation but has been skilfully restored by the Ministry of the Environment to a place of quiet peace and beauty.

RHU [Row]. *See* Campbell, J. McLeod.

RICHARDSON, Andrew. *See* Gillespie, Thomas.

ROBE, John. *See* Cambuslang.

ROBERTSON, William B. 1820–86. Minister of Trinity U.P. Church, Irvine and one of the outstanding preachers of his day; in a minor way, also a poet. His sermons are among the few from last century which are still readable; in delivery and content he broke from Secession tradition. It is obvious that consciously or unconsciously later preachers such as Morrison, Gossip and Hubert Simpson, owed much to Robertson. He had passing contact with greatness in the person of Thomas de Quincey, who in one of his bleakest periods had taken refuge from his creditors at the home of his lawyer McIndoe in Princes Street. He refused to come out of his room or see anyone and had his food passed in to him. The exception he made was the young relative of the McIndoe's, Robertson, who was studying at the divinity hall and whom he invited in for long conversations. Robertson later acknowledged the debt he owed for this stimulating intellectual contact and the older man must have developed more than a passing interest in the student, for when Robertson was in his charge at Irvine he received a sudden call from de Quincey who was staying in Glasgow. As related by Page, de Quincey's biographer, the minister was out visiting and his housekeeper refused to allow the unkempt little man over the threshold to write a note. Robertson later denied that any discourtesy had been shown and said that the Opium Eater had written apologizing for not giving warning of his call. Unfortunately neither man seems to have made any further effort to correspond or meet. Considering that de Quincey refused to leave his Edinburgh

fireside to walk 200 yards to meet the famous novelist Thackeray, Robertson of Irvine might have felt proud that he travelled so far to meet him.

ROBERTSON SMITH, William. 1846–1894. He is to be classed among those who have been martyred by their own generation for holding views which a century later would be universally accepted. Educated at home by his father, an Aberdeenshire Free Church minister, and later at Aberdeen and Edinburgh, he was in 1870 appointed Professor of Hebrew and Old Testament at Aberdeen, where he might have spent a life of leisured study had it not been for the controversy which broke upon the Church at this time concerning the infallibility of scripture. The young scholar had met the German critic Wellhausen at Gottingen and listened to his application of scientific literary critical methods to the Bible. Did a theory of inspiration demand a belief that the very words were dictated by God? Were there not varying and even contradictory accounts of incidents such as the Flood? Were the first books actually written by Moses? Other scholars were well aware of the problems and of the criticism but it fell to Robertson Smith to kindle the controversy by his articles in the *Encyclopaedia Britannica*. James Begg† led the attack; Rainy† defended and then, fearing for division within his Church, turned his coat. Smith presented such a spirited defence in the Assembly that a spectator wrote 'Begg's ruddy countenance blanched for once.' He won the first round but in 1881 the Free Church removed him from his chair. Rainy's sacrifice of Robertson Smith to save his Church from division failed, for in 1892 a group of Highland ministers and students left to form the F.P. Church, and in 1900 a larger group remained outside the Union with the U.Ps., retaining the name Free Church but universally known as Wee Frees. Robertson Smith's reputation as a scholar was in no way diminished by his trials at the hands of the Free Church; he subsequently became Professor of Arabic and University librarian at Cambridge. He died, prematurely worn out, at 42, re-living in his delirium the agony of his arraignment and crying out 'Moderator, Moderator!'

ROSE, Hugh, of Kilravock. The hereditary barons of Kilravock (pronounced Kilroak) have always been Hugh, so the only method of distinguishing them is by numbers. In 1220 Hugh Rose of Geddes, a village near Cawdor not far from the Roses' later castle, dedicated a chapel to the Holy Virgin where masses were to be sung in perpetuity for the Rose clan, an act for which his descendants would give him little thanks for they became Protestants and Covenanters. About 1530 Kilravock IX anticipated the Reformation by imprisoning the Abbot of Kinloss in his dungeon — a not too unpleasant little dungeon as befitted a Christian family — but he himself suffered a longer imprisonment in Dumbarton Castle. Hugh X, the Black Baron, welcomed both Mary of Scots and James VI to his castle but managed to remain safe and uncommitted during the civil strife. It was the XIIth Baron and his younger brother, William, Provost of Nairn, who threw in their lot with the Covenanting cause; Hugh signed the National Covenant when it was brought to Inverness, while William was a member of the General Assembly which abolished Episcopacy. 'Non est salus nisi in Christo' was the tablet which the latter put on the bridge he had built for Nairn. With the Restoration came the second covenanting period and Kilravock XIV joined Brodie of Brodie and other local lairds in resisting the king's demands even at the cost of heavy fines and loss of lands. His good wife, Margaret Innes, was one of the leading women of the Covenant and the castle's secret chamber shielded many ministers and others. She died at the age of 36 and was given the simple epitaph that 'she disturbed not the public peace.' Kilravock, which stands on the Croy road not many miles from Culloden, was visited just before the battle by both the Prince and the Duke but the Hugh Rose of the day took no sides and was found, spade in hand, tending his garden. The last Hugh was killed tragically at El Alamein at the age of 20 before he succeeded to Kilravock, and the present Kilravock XXV is Elizabeth Rose who has maintained the evangelical traditions of her family and opened the old castle as a Christian guest-house, turning the granary and outbuildings into a Conference Centre

for youth.

ROSEMARKIE. *See* Curitan.

ROSNEATH CHURCH (Dunbarton). The dedication, St Modan's, is quite recent; there is nothing to connect the Celtic saint with this parish. The site dates from the twelfth century when it is recorded under the patronage of Paisley Abbey, but the present building — one of the most seemly of Scottish village churches — dates only from 1853. There is a tradition that John Balfour of Burley, one of the assassins of Archbishop Sharp, was buried in the kirkyard under the name of Andrew Salter. Notable nineteenth century ministers of the parish were Robert Story, responsible for the new church, his son Robert H. Story, chaplain to Queen Victoria, Professor of Church History and then Principal of Glasgow University (*see* Primmer, Jacob) and Alfred Warr, father of Charles L. Warr, the future minister of St Giles and Dean of the Order of the Thistle. After his deposition, McLeod Campbell† lived in Rosneath and is buried in the graveyard.

ROW [Rhu]. *See* Campbell, J. McLeod.

RULE [Regulus]. It is impossible to put a date to a saint so hypothetical and legendary. There were two Irish saints or missionaries of the name Riaghuil, one of whom was of Muc Innis (Pig Isle) on the Shannon, the place associated earlier with the name of Cainnech, or Kenneth. The mediaeval story was that one Regulus sailed from Greece with relics of the Apostle Andrew and was wrecked on the coast at Kilrymont. The monkish chroniclers were adept at combining legends, particularly in order to secure apostolic connection with their foundation. In this story it is possible that the Irish Riaghuil (pronounced Rule) has been introduced in the form Regulus to link the earlier Celtic Church with the later Roman diocese. There is some reason to believe that Kenneth† laboured in the district and should have the honour of being patron, and in the version given above we note that while he is overlooked it is his successor at Muc Innis who is introduced in a very changed role. There is, it has to be admitted, very little evidence to suggest that the cave beside St Andrews Castle, once visited by Dr Johnson and called St Rule's, ever sheltered a hermit of that name, and the great Pictish-type tower standing so incongruously in the shadow of the cathedral, is still much of a mystery not only in the reason for its name, but for its purpose and date.

RULLION GREEN. *See* Peden, Alexander.

RUTHERFORD, Samuel. 1600–61. Leading theologian and apologist on the covenanting side. His controversial *Lex Rex* (The Law is the King) was condemned as treasonable. He seems to have been elected Professor of Divinity at Edinburgh at the age of 23 but for some scandal or irregularity left at 26. The incident is vague and if he was guilty of some serious offence it would have been extremely unlikely that he would have been chosen as parish minister of Anwoth (Stewartry of Kirkcudbright) in the following year (1627). The ruins of his church still stand today a mile or so inland from the Solway shore. After nine years he was deposed for his political views and banished to Aberdeen where he hated the prevailing episcopacy. On the death of King Charles he was made Professor of Divinity at St Andrews and became Principal of St Mary's College in 1649. His *Letters* are perhaps the nearest thing to mystical-devotional literature that presbyterianism has produced despite the flames of controversy and persecution in which they were written. On the Restoration of the Stewarts he was cited before Parliament for high-treason but died before he could appear: 'I behove to obey my first summons.'

RUTHWELL CROSS (Dumfriesshire; AM). Standing within the parish church of Ruthwell (pronounced Rivvel) is this most noble of all runic or Northumbrian crosses, of date *c.* 680, possibly set up by Colman of Lindisfarne†, who held to the Celtic rather than the Roman usage after the Synod of Whitby and returned to Scotland. It is a preaching cross, erected to mark the place assigned for the message of the Gospel, and showing in its panels scenes from scripture. It has, in addition to texts in Latin script, lines of runes. For long these defied translation, but they are now known to be parts

of the Anglo-Saxon poem on the crucifixion:

'Then the young hero, he was God Almighty, firm and unflinching,
Stripped himself. He mounted on the high cross-beam in the sight of many when he was minded to redeem mankind. Then I trembled when the Hero clasped me, yet I durst not bow to the earth, fall to the level of the ground, but I must needs stand firm.'

In 1640 the General Assembly decreed the demolition of 'idolatrous monuments, crucifixes, images etc. . . .' and the local presbytery forced the minister of Ruthwell, Gavin Young, to cast the monument down. He was, fortunately, reasonably gentle with it and it was laid along the kirk floor, perhaps to act as seats. The great cross transom, was however, broken and eventually lost. When the church was enlarged the shaft was taken outside and erected from its pieces in the manse garden. In 1887 it was taken into care as an Ancient Monument and replaced in the Church in a special apse built for it. Unfortunately one section has been misplaced and the replacement of the top and arms which were lost is somewhat spoilt by masonic emblems which were no part of the original. *See also* Duncan, Henry.

ST ANDREWS (Fife). *See* Beaton; Knox; Melville; Rule; Spottiswoode.

ST ANDREW CHAPEL, EDINBURGH. *See* Barclay, John.

ST ANDREW'S EPISCOPAL CHURCH, MILLPORT. *See* Cumbrae.

ST ANDREW'S PARISH CHURCH, DUNDEE. *See* Glas, John.

ST ANDREW'S PARISH CHURCH, DUNFERMLINE. *See* Gillespie Church.

ST ASAPH'S (Llanelwy). *See* Kentigern.

ST BRIDE'S EPISCOPAL CHURCH, LOCHABER. *See* Chinnery-Haldane.

ST COLUMBA'S FREE CHURCH, EDINBURGH. *See* Guthrie, Thomas.

ST GEORGE'S EPISCOPAL CHAPEL, EDINBURGH. *See* Ramsay, Edward.

ST GILES' CATHEDRAL (The High Kirk of Edinburgh). *See* Durie, John; Giles; Knox, John; Spottiswoode, John.

ST GILES' CHURCH, ELGIN. *See* Giles.

ST JOHN'S EPISCOPAL CHURCH, BALLACHULISH. *See* Chinnery-Haldane.

ST JOHN'S EPISCOPAL CHURCH, EDINBURGH. *See* Ramsay, Edward.

ST JOHN'S EPISCOPAL CHURCH, PERTH. *See* Wordsworth, Charles.

ST JOHN'S FREE CHURCH, EDINBURGH. *See* Guthrie, Thomas.

ST KATHARINE'S CONVENT, EDINBURGH. *See* Sciennes.

ST MARGARET'S, BARNHILL. *See* Primmer, Jacob.

ST MARGARET'S CONVENT, EDINBURGH. *See* Trail, Ann Agnes.

ST MARY'S CATHOLIC GIRLS SCHOOL, EDINBURGH. *See* Trail, Ann Agnes.

ST MARYS CHAPEL, NIDDRY'S WYND, EDINBURGH. *See* Maxwell. Willielma.

ST MARY'S EPISCOPAL CATHEDRAL, EDINBURGH. This imposing neo-gothic building was the gift of the Misses Mary and Barbara Walker and may be considered either as one of the capital's monstrous mistakes — for it clashes horribly with the Georgian severity of the surrounding streets — or as one of the best examples of late nineteenth century gothic in Scotland, which, if we view it alone, it is. How wonderful the effect of a classical cathedral — a Scottish St Paul's — might have been we shall never know, for St Mary's dates from the time when many Episcopalians considered that to worship beneath anything other than pointed arches was almost disrespect to the Faith. They had some excuse for this view as chancel, nave and transepts were functionally suited to their liturgy; but, strangely, the same love for modern gothic infected the United Free Church in a delayed reaction of some years, and the wealthier districts and suburbs of most Scottish towns became dotted with spires and arched doorways externally, and internally with chancels which were not functional to the presbyterian service as generally practised.

Two notable Bishops of the Edinburgh Episcopal diocese were Dowden†, an Irishman, and Walpole who came from Cornwall and was father of the novelist, Hugh Walpole.

ST MARY'S EPISCOPAL CHURCH, BROUGHTY FERRY. *See* Erskine, Thomas.

ST MARY'S EPISCOPAL CHURCH, GLENCOE. *See* Chinnery-Haldane.

ST NINIAN'S CATHEDRAL, PERTH. *See* Wordsworth, Charles.

ST PAUL'S CATHEDRAL, DUNDEE. *See* Forbes, Alexander.

ST PAUL'S CHURCH, NEWINGTON, EDINBURGH. *See* Begg, James.

ST PETER'S EPISCOPAL CHURCH, EDINBURGH. *See* Sciennes.

ST PETER'S ROMAN CATHOLIC CHURCH, ABERDEEN. *See* Gordon, Charles.

ST ROQUE'S CHAPEL, EDINBURGH. *See* Sciennes.

ST VIGEAN'S (Angus). *See* Drostan.

SANDEMAN, Robert. *See* Glas, John.

SANDFORD, Daniel. *See* Ramsay, Edward.

SANDILANDS, Sir James (Lord Torphichen). *See* Torphichen.

SAUCHIEBURN (Kincardineshire). *See* Barclay, John.

SCALAN (Banffshire). From 1717 to 1799 a secret seminary for priests was held in what was little more than a hut on the remote uplands of this small county. A short-lived attempt at a college on an island in Loch Morar was broken up after the 1715 Rising and two years later, Dr Gordon, coadjutor to Bishop Nicholson, first Roman Catholic bishop in Scotland since the Reformation, made a fresh start at Scalan on the Duke of Gordon's estate. The first building was of turf and was twice pulled down by the military, and when it was rebuilt in stone in 1738 it still could hold no more than 15 students. It was again destroyed after the '45, and again it was rebuilt. Commissioners from the

Scalan Seminary

General Assembly, sent to visit it, reported it to be so mean that they did not trouble to dismount to inspect it. It was here that in penal days the Scottish bishops met and for long it was the centre of the Lowland District. Bishop Hay† was consecrated here in 1769 and here, with a special dispensation, he alone consecrated Alexander Macdonald as new Bishop for the Highland Vicariate, without the usual other two bishops. Before it was supplanted by Aquhorties in 1799, over 100 priests had been trained at Scalan. Most of these went on to complete their studies at one of the continental Scots Colleges — Douai, Paris, Lisbon, Valladolid or Rome — but for others, commonly known as 'heather priests', this was their only seminary. In its later years Scalan was supervised by Bishop Hay who secured more accessible but still unpretentious premises at Aquhorties in the Don valley which served the Lowland District until the removal to Blairs† in 1829.

SCHOOL WYND CHURCH, DUNDEE.
See Gilfillan, George.

SCIENNES, EDINBURGH. A corruption of Siena. 'Marmion', looking down from Blackford Hill calls the convent 'St Katharine's of Sienne' (Canto IV. 31) while Sir David Lindsay, finding no corrup-

tion in their house, makes Chastity flee for refuge to 'the Sisteris of the Schenis'. Founded in 1517 by Lady Seton, whose husband had been killed at Flodden, the buildings stood on the south of the Boroughloch, approximately on the site of the present St Catherine's Place. At the gateway from Causewayside stood a small Chapel of St John Baptist which had been erected only five years earlier by Sir John Crawford who himself officiated in his chapel and acted as chaplain to the nuns. The donation deed stipulated that the chaplain should always be of his name or family and should wear a white cassock with a portraiture of St John Baptist. The first Prioress of the convent, Josina Henryson, maintained strict discipline and no breath of scandal was ever raised against the community. In 1544 it suffered in the English attack on the city, and after being rebuilt enjoyed just over 20 years of active life until the Reformers drove out the nuns and destroyed the building. Grant (*Old and New Edinburgh* vol. iii) gives woodcuts of 1854 showing considerable remains which were then used as sheepfolds, but by the time he wrote they were almost all away. In the seventeenth century the ruins had been used as a burial place for plague victims from the city and this may have given rise to the story that the nuns cared for the diseased who had been put outside the walls to die. This act of mercy should more properly be attributed to St Roque's Chapel, further west on the Boroughmuir. In Sciennes Hill House, now scarcely distinguishable from the tenements of Sciennes House Place (formerly Braid Place) Burns and Scott had their famous meeting at the home of Professor Adam Ferguson. Later the house passed into the hands of John Biggar, who ran a prosperous linen manufactory in the Sciennes. His son, grand-son and great-grand-son, all Johns, became architects and the second John Biggar is notable in the history of St Peter's Episcopal Church. Originally of the Established Kirk, he was disillusioned by the Disruption and became a keen Episcopalian and member of the Vestry of St Peter's, then in Roxburgh Place. He was instrumental in gathering funds for a new church in Lutton Place and his son, the third John Biggar, supervised its erection although the design was not from his board.

SCOTT, Andrew. 1772–1846. Roman Catholic Bishop of Glasgow, to whom is due the cathedral fronting the Clyde. Born in the Enzie of Banff, educated at Scalan† and Douai, whence he had to return because of the French Revolution (along with Priest Gordon†). Ordained by Bishop Hay† in 1795, priest at Dee Castle and at Huntly, he came to Glasgow in 1805. Until 20 years earlier there had been only a handful of Catholics in that town — in 1677 they numbered 50 and were down to 30 a century later. Now two factors led to a sudden increase: the beginning of Irish immigration and the Highland clearances which brought many of the dispersed Catholics into the town. Mr Scott (the title Father at that time was applied only to the 'regular' not the 'secular' clergy) came to a little chapel in the Calton, opposite the barracks, where the protection of the military was reassuring in the times of the frequent riots. For the first decade of his Glasgow priesthood he laboured to collect money for the proposed new chapel in Clyde Street which he hoped might be the largest and most beautiful place of Catholic worship in the country. The architect was to be James Gillespie Graham. Most dissenting places of worship in those days were called 'chapel' but from about 1839 it was called 'church' and it became 'cathedral' in 1885. Mr Scott was a controversialist and Glasgow witnessed a long battle between himself and a Glasgow merchant named William McGavin, one of the long line of militant Protestants the city has produced. McGavin was prosecuted for slander and, when he lost, the compensation went towards the building fund against which he was protesting. But there were also many tokens of goodwill and understanding from Protestants such as Kirkman Finlay, M.P. Thomas Chalmers† preached a sermon in aid of the schools for Catholic children which Finlay had helped the Glasgow priest to establish. In 1828 the Glasgow Herald announced 'Our very respectable Catholic clergyman, the Rev. Andrew Scott, was invested with the ecclesiastical title of Bishop.' It was the first Catholic episcopal consecration in the city since the Reformation.

SCOTT, James. See Keiss.

SEABURY, Samuel. See Skinner, John.

SEGINE. See Adamnan; Aidan.

SELKIRK. See Kelso.

SERF [Servanus, Serb, perhaps Ternan]. Fifth–sixth century. The dating of this Celtic missionary is so confused that the Bollandist scholars (*Acta Sanctorum*) suggest he may be a conflation of two or even three distinct persons. It is claimed that Palladius consecrated him bishop, but this might simply be an attempt to secure a Roman succession for the Celtic Church; it would make him almost contemporary with Patrick†. He is by others represented as contemporary with Adamnan†, almost 300 years later. The traditional story, made up from various scraps of mediaeval 'Vitae' and rendered into doggerel verse by Wyntoun in his *Cronykil*, places him chronologically between the two extremes. He is said to have fostered and educated Kentigern† at Culross, but we have suggested that a more likely place for Serf's 'muinntir' or community could be Airthrey (Logie Airth†). It is here that Wyntoun places Serf's pet lamb:

'This haly man had a ram
That he had fed wp off a lame

And oysyd hym to folow aye
Quhare-ewyre he passyd in hys way;
A theffe this schepe in Athren stall
And ete hym wp in pesis small. . . .'

The suspect denies the crime,

'Bot sone he worthyd rede for schame,
The schepe thare bletyd in hys wame.'

'Wame' of course means 'stomach'. Not far along the foothills is Tillicoultry where:

'In Twlycultry till a wiffe
Twa swnnys he rasyd fra dede to lyff.'

In the next village, Alva, the saint's well, formerly in the glebe of the church which is dedicated to him, has been covered by a housing estate where the house reputedly above it is said to be damp. The church at Tullibody and several others in the area have Serf dedications. One mediaeval narrative credits him with being 'the apostle of the Orkneys', obviously an error for Ochils. In addition to the above examples, the saint's bridge is in Glendevon, Fossoway is his parish, at Dunning (where later he is said to have died) he fought a dragon at a spot still remembered; the motto of Auchtermuchty, DUM SERO SPERO is an obvious pun on his name. His desertum or retreat is at Dysart; St Serf's Island, in Loch Leven, has the ruin of a later Priory which supplanted the earlier Culdee buildings. Wyntoun himself lived there.

SETON, Janet, Lady. See Sciennes.

SHALLOCH ON MINNOCH (Ayrshire). Desolate high moor bordering Galloway and Carrick, north of the Merrick. Here the Society Men, the extreme Covenanters, held their conventicles in 'The Killing Times'. 'There is not much to be seen,' writes S. R. Crockett (see Balmaghie Church), who weaves the place into his novel *Men of The Moss Hags*, 'but all the air is sacred, pregnant with history, and to stand on the Session Stone with the ranged seats opposite and the white stones of the parched burn beneath brings the times that were in Scotland wondrously near to us.'

SHARP, John. See Blairs College.

SHIELDAIG. See Macfarlane, Donald.

SHIELDS, Alexander. See Renwick, James.

SHORT, George. See Balmaghie Church.

SIMPSON, Elspeth ['Luckie' Buchan]. 1738–91. The Scottish Joanna Southcote. Her story is included here to show the unbelievable credulity of some religious folk. Born at Cornhill, near Banff, orphaned, she was brought up by a lady described as 'a loose episcopalian'. When her mistress emigrated to Jamaica, Elspeth wandered to Glasgow, where she met and married Robert Buchan, a potter at Delftfield, who secured for her a post as servant to his employer. They had three children but Buchan found that city life was not the best for his flighty spouse and he packed her off with the family to Banff where she ran a dame school. As a girl she had a vivid religious imagination and now she began to experience prophetic ecstasies. Returning to Glasgow she formed a partnership with Hugh White, a Relief minister with a somewhat unusual clerical career. Claiming to be the Woman Clothed with the Sun (Revelation 12), she declared she had borne White as her spiritual man-child, and, as in the prophecy, they would be driven into the wilderness for time, times and half a time. At Irvine they formed a commune of some 50 souls, holding goods in common and refusing to marry or beget children. Popular feeling against them became so strong that they were driven from the town and crossed the high moors into the Nith valley, singing

'We march and we sound our trumpets around.
We'll all in short time in sweet glory be found.'

They were offered shelter in a barn near Closeburn, and as they were good workers, took no personal wages and were useful to the farmer, he allowed them to remain and the barn became known as Buchan Hall. In July 1786 the three and a half years of the prophecy were accomplished and after a fast of 40 days, during which they threw away watches, rings and shoes so that they might more easily rise, they moved across to Templand Hill to await the end of the world. All night they stood singing beside the platform they had erected for 'Friend Mother in the Lord'; unfortunately a storm arose and the watching crowd (which is said to have included Robert Burns from nearby Ellisland) saw the prophetess tumbled among her followers as the platform collapsed. Some left after this disappointment but the others were ordered by the county authorities to move on, and they used the money they had saved in the community to rent the farm of Auchengibbert in Urr parish. Dressed in uniform green frocks and smocks the women and the men worked for neighbouring farmers and were well spoken-of. But within the community White was now openly disbelieving and often quarrelling with Friend Mother. In 1791, to their surprise, she died, for they had expected she would live on. On her death-bed she prophesied that she would return in six days if their faith were strong enough; if not, it would be ten years; if not then — it would finally come to pass on the fiftieth anniversary. Before long, White led 30 off to Portpatrick en route for America; the remainder took a small upland farm at Larghill. Although, officially, Mrs Buchan had been buried in Kirkgunzeon kirkyard, Andrew Innes† her most devoted follower, had preserved the corpse in feathers and kept it beneath the hearthstone. Ten years passed without her rising. The community, now dwindled to a dozen, moved to Crocketford to a two-storeyed house, which today is a 'bed-and-breakfast' and which until recently had a large portrait of Andrew Innes in the hall. By the final resurrection date, 1841, only Innes and Katie Gardner, who was in effect his wife, were left. When he died in 1846 the mummified Luckie was buried below him at the back of the house where six other Buchanites lay — and still lie.

SINCLAIR, Sir William. *See* Keiss.

SKINNER, John. 1774–1816. Bishop of Aberdeen in the Scottish Episcopal Church, consecrated almost secretly in 1782 in the chapel at Luthermuir in the Mearns. The elder John Skinner, known as the poet-priest of Linshart, was a convert from Presbyterianism who had been ordained by the much-travelled, ardent Jacobite Robert Forbes. At the age of nine the younger Skinner had accompanied his father to prison in Old Aberdeen for a breach of the penal laws. The third generation produced a second Bishop of Aberdeen in the person of William Skinner, John's eldest son, while another son, a third John, became Dean of Brechin. Bishop John Skinner, with Bishops Kilgour and Petrie, officiated at the consecration of Samuel Seabury to be first bishop of the Episcopal Church in America. The ceremony was carried out in Skinner's house in Longacre, Aberdeen. English bishops felt that because of their position in the establishment they would have had to put to him the oath of loyalty to King George. The Scottish bishops, disestablished, were under no such obligation.

SMITH, James. *See* Balchrystie.

SOULSEAT (by Castle Kennedy, Wigtownshire). Sited by a small, algae-infested loch which probably inspired the name *Viride Stagnum*, no other mediaeval abbey has been so completely obliterated so that no physical trace remains. The alternative title, *Sedes Animarum* (souls' seat), may be a corruption of Saul's Seat, suggesting the foundation by a body of monks fleeing from Sabhull (Saul) in Co. Down. There is a tradition that the founder was an abbot named Saul which could possibly be a variant of this memory. We know that around 1150 Soulseat was founded as the first Premonstratensian house in Scotland and that its abbot held primacy over the Order, even over the more famous Dryburgh† founded about the same time. In Bernard of Clairvaux's account of the life of St Malachy [Maelmadoc], the founder of the Cistercians in Ireland, there is mention of the founding of a house of the Cistercians in the year of Malachy's death (1148) at a place in Wigtownshire called *Viride Stagnum*. This has been identified with Soulseat but if this be the case what became of these monks if so soon afterwards it was filled with Premonstratensians? It is just possible that the identification was wrong and referred to some other place — but if so we are left with an extra abbey to place somewhere! It is not too fanciful to suspect that Soulseat might have an Ulster connection even older than Malachy, perhaps in some way linked to the 'Solway mission' of Patrick and his successors.

SOUTH CHURCH, DUNDEE. *See* Willison, John.

SOUTH LEITH PARISH CHURCH, EDINBURGH. *See* Restalrig.

SPOTTISWOODE, John. 1565–1639. Son of one of the same name who became one of Knox's superintendents. John Spottiswoode the younger was called to London to receive episcopal consecration. The proceedings raise interesting problems with regard to church order. Spottiswoode was already a 'Presbyter' of Ecclesia Scoticana but, after Presbyterian fashion, had been ordained not by Bishops but by Presbyters — who, of course, in Presbyterian eyes were also Bishops. Bancroft, Archbishop of Canterbury, ruled that 'where bishops could not be had, the ordination given by presbyters must be esteemed lawful, otherwise it might be doubted if there were any lawful ordination in most of the Reformed Churches.' Apparently within a few years the opposite view prevailed, for Leighton† was compelled to suffer reordination as Presbyter. The ceremony might also have raised the question of the superiority of the English over the Scottish Church if consecration had been by the Archbishops, but the king with foresight had arranged that it be performed by three simple diocesans. Spottiswoode was made Archbishop of Glasgow and then Primate at St Andrews. He was Moderator of the General Assembly at Perth in 1618 and secured the safe passage of James's 'Black Articles'. He crowned Charles I at Holyrood and was present in St Giles' when the new liturgy was introduced and the famous stool was thrown. He was made Lord Chancellor of Scotland, an act of the king which roused much opposition as the post had not been offered to a cleric since the Reformation. He compiled a history of the Church of Scotland which is a standard work. If we forget his embroilment in church politics which made him so hated we can enjoy the real beauty of the little church which he built at Dairsie 'after the English pattern'. It stands on an eminence on the road to Dura Den, not far from the castle which the Archbishop also owned. Spottiswoode's arms are still on the church porch.

SPROTT, George W. *See* Lee, Robert.

STEWART, Allan. *See* Crossraguel.

STIRLING (Chapel Royal). *See* Angus, John.

STOBHALL (Perthshire). Ancient estate of the Drummonds, north of Perth on A93. Remembered by Catholics as one of the oldest of their 'missions' in the days before emancipation. At a time when regularly organized congregations in towns would have been impossible, even had numbers justified them, ministrations were in many cases centred on the homes of Catholic noblemen who maintained a chapel and chaplain. Such a family were the Drummonds of Drummond Castle and Stobhall, whose head later bore the title Earl of Perth. One Andrew Hacket is recorded as serving as priest at Stobhall early in the eighteenth century; he had been ordained at Rome in 1708. A catechism compiled by him was publicly burned at Edinburgh Cross. Notable among the lairds who furthered the Stobhall mission was Jean, daughter of the Duke of Gordon and wife of the fifth Earl of Perth; an ardent Jacobite, she managed to retain Stobhall when the Drummond estates were attainted. By some mischance she did not will the chapel and estates to the Church and so they passed to the Crown Commissioners, but they were not unfriendly and contributed material towards the building of a 'mass house'. In the winter of 1778 an example of friendly relations with the Protestant neighbours occurred when, during an outburst of sectarian feeling in Perth, an excited mob of 'Friends to Protestantism' set out to attack the settlement, only to be confronted by a large force of the neighbours' servants armed and ready to do battle. Abbé Macpherson, priest at Stobhall from 1783 to 1792, saw the Drummond estate restored and a chapel and priest's house built. His work covered a wide area — Dundee, Montrose, Perth and most of Fife. The last priest, William Rattray, a convert from Protestantism, removed to Dundee in 1824 as Irish immigration had greatly increased the Catholic population in that town. He returned to say mass at Stobhall only at intervals and on his death in 1827 the mission was given up.

STORY, ROBERT. *See* Primmer, Jacob; Rosneath.

STRATHKINNESS (Fife). *See* Kenneth; Ward, Valentine.

STRUTHERS, James P. 1851–1915. A considerable scholar, Greek medallist at Glasgow, who, when he left college, refused the offer of a chair of Greek at an Australian university. 'What,' said Dr Caird, through whom the offer was made, 'will you reject this to become a Cameronian minister at £80 a year?' But he did, and later he consistently refused the offer of D.D. from his own university. He became Cameronian, or Reformed Presbyterian, minister at Whithorn, a tiny congregation in a remote if lovely little village. Later he moved to Greenock where he ministered for the rest of his life. Here he became famous far beyond the bounds of his own little denomination — Struthers of Greenock, powerful in preaching, most kindly of men, and editor of *The Morning Watch*, a halfpenny magazine for children. Nearly half a century later H. R. Mackintosh used to warn his students never to allow a copy to lie on a second-hand book-stall: 'Buy it and have a complete set in your library'. With

none of the professional 'know-how' Struthers was a great journalist, getting across his message week by week and year by year. The Church he loved and served was the successor to the gatherings of Society Men or Cameronians. They had never become part of the national Presbyterian church. Cameron and Shields had led them in covenanting days, and later Macmillan of Balmaghie† had given them form as the Reformed Presbyterian Church. In 1876 the majority united with the Free Church (*see* City Temple, Edinburgh) but Struthers was one of those who remained with the remnant, and in spite of unions there remains today a handful of R.P. congregations in Scotland, and some over in Ulster.

SWEETHEART ABBEY (New Abbey, Dumfriesshire; AM). One of the group of Galloway Cistercian Abbeys and the last to be founded, and so called New Abbey to distinguish it from Dundrennan. John Baliol, who came to Galloway from Barnard Castle, died in 1267 and his widow Devorgilla had his heart embalmed and

Sweetheart Abbey

placed in a silver casket which she took with her wherever she went. At meals the heart was set beside her and portions of food were placed before it, to be given afterwards to the poor. She had the Abbey built so that on her death she and the heart might rest within its walls, a wish which was accomplished. She died at Barnard Castle, the heart was placed on her bosom, and the White Monks carried it on its long journey to its resting place beside the high altar of the New Abbey. When they saw the Reformation coming the monks sought security for their property by placing it under the protection of the powerful Maxwell family. The last Abbot, Gilbert Browne remained loyal to the 'old faith' and worked for a Catholic reaction. The Assembly of 1594 demanded his apprehension — 'The perverting papist . . . quho evir since the reformatioun of religioun had conteinit in ignorance . . . allmost the haill south west partis of Scotland . . .' He was imprisoned in Blackness Castle and later in Edinburgh, but was allowed to go free; after he had left Edinburgh for Paris 'his masse clothes, chalices etc. were found by the bailliffes.' Considerable remains of the Abbey still stand. The old bridge over the Nith at Dumfries bears Devorgilla's name.

SWINTON, John. *See* Barclay, Robert.

SYNOD HALL, EDINBURGH. *See* Cairns, John.

TAIT, Archibald Campbell. 1811–82. Edinburgh High School and Academy, Glasgow and Oxford Universities; successively Tutor at Balliol, Head of Rugby, Dean of Carlisle, Bishop of London, Archbishop of Canterbury. Born in Park Place, Edinburgh. His father, Crauford Tait, an Edinburgh Writer, had inherited Harviestoun, near Dollar (*see* Mylne, Andrew). As a baby Archie Tait suffered from such badly deformed feet that it was feared he might be a lifelong cripple but he was cured by a remarkable blacksmith of Rochdale, John Taylor, who included royalty among his patients. Although of Aberdeenshire Episcopalian background all Tait's immediate family were Presbyterian, but at Oxford he was confirmed and took Anglican orders. Despite the fact that all his lifework was to lie south of the

Border he never lost his Scottish friends and interests. He was ungraciously dubbed 'the Presbyterian Bishop' when he refused to accept the Anglo-Catholic interpretation of the Church as excluding all but confirmed Episcopalians. He was himself intensely loyal to the Church of his choosing and refused to stand for the chair of Moral Philosophy at Glasgow as he would have had to subscribe to the Westminster Confession. At Rugby he had the difficult task of following the great Arnold and did not leave any deep impression as Headmaster. In 1849, following a serious illness, he was offered the Carlisle deanery as a less exacting post. In seven years there he effected complete restoration of the fabric of this smallest of English cathedrals. He and his wife suffered a domestic tragedy which shocked the nation: within a few weeks five of their seven children were struck down by scarlet fever and buried in Stanwix churchyard. Over 60 years later, when the present writer was a boy in Carlisle, memory of the tragedy was still fresh in the city and the graves of the five little girls were still visited. In the same year, perhaps as a result of the Queen's sympathy, Tait was appointed to the see of London, the first metropolitan bishop to be appointed direct from a deanery for over two centuries. At Fulham his policy was a moderation which was little pleasing to extremists on either side. At Oxford he stood out against the Tractarians, criticizing what he regarded as the incipient Romanism of Tract Ninety. Now at London he had support from some of the same Tractarians in opposing the Ritualists — auricular confession, coloured vestments, altar candles were at that date novelties in Anglican churches and Tait showed little sympathy with the innovators. On the other hand, when called on to intervene in the controversy on liberal theology and scriptural inspiration he roused the wrath of the Evangelicals. As Primate, for he was appointed to Canterbury in 1868, he was able to hold the Church together during difficult years of controversy when under a more extreme archbishop it might have split in two. He possessed tact, firmness but sincere piety: qualities needed at the time. He was offered burial in the Abbey but at the desire of his family was interred in Addington Church-yard, although Dollar people are convinced he lies in 'Tait's Tomb', a large walled enclosure opposite the · entrance to the former Harviestoun house where Crauford Tait and others of the family are buried. Tait's moderate policies were continued by his son-in-law biographer Randall David-son, also a Scot of mingled Presbyterian-Episcopalian background, who himself ruled at Canterbury for 25 years before giving place to another Scotsman, Cosmo Gordon Lang.

TAIT, Crauford. *See* Mylne, Andrew; Tait, Archibald.

TANNADICE. *See* Adamnan.

TANTALLON CASTLE. *See* Hickhorn-gill, Edward.

TEALING. *See* Curitan; Glas, John.

THENEW [Enoch, Denw, Thanay] *fl. c.* 520? Traditionally daughter of Loth [Leudonus], king of Lothian, and mother of Kentigern†. Wooed by Ewen [Owein] son of Urien, one of the great Brittonic heroes, she became pregnant. There are differing versions of the incident: some suggested a virgin birth, but this was con-sidered sacrilegious, others that Ewen dis-guised himself as a maiden to deceive her; in other versions a mysterious swineherd complicates the story. It is obvious that the variants are all attempts to preserve her honour. Her father, however, was not satisfied and decreed death, but whether for unchastity or because she had chosen the swineherd and not the prince is un-certain. An attempt to send her hurtling down Dunpelder (Traprain Law) in a chariot was unsuccessful when the shafts caught in the rocks where you can see the scrape marks (glaciation?) today. She was then cast off in an open boat from Aber-lessic (Aberlady? or Tyninghame?). The craft floated out past May Island but was supported by a shoal of fishes and carried up the Forth to land at Culross just as the baby was born. Dunpelder is said to have associations with Modwenna or Triduana and Thenew might have been one of her maids. The whole story is fanciful but may have arisen from a tradition which refused to be suppressed that Kentigern was illegitimate. Being cast off in an open boat is a Celtic myth with psychological under-tones, told of many figures (*see Ulster Journal of Archaeology*, Vol. 27, article by E. S. Towill on St Mochaoi). She was said to have followed her saintly son to Glasgow where she is buried either in the cathedral or beside what is now St Enoch's Under-ground station. *See also* Restalrig.

THURSO. *See* Dick, Robert.

TILLICOULTRY (Clackmannanshire). *See* Serf.

TORPHICHEN, Preceptory of (West Lothian). The Knights Hospitallers of St John of Jerusalem, founded in the eleventh century to serve poor and sick pilgrims,

took upon themselves the more exciting task of the defence of the Holy Sepulchre and the defeat of the infidels and so they became more a military than a monkish order. The Hospital or Preceptory of Torphichen is still their substantial memo-rial in Scotland. Dating from the twelfth century it looks more like a castle than a church. The nave has disappeared under the seventeenth century parish church and most of the remaining mediaeval work is of the thirteenth to fifteenth centuries. The last preceptor, Sir James Sandilands, received the lands and title of Lord Torphichen in return for joining the Reformers. There is a modern revival of the Knights with more peaceable aims than their predecessors.

TOWNHILL (Dunfermline, Fife). *See* Primmer, Jacob.

TRAIL, Ann Agnes [Sister Agnes Xavier]. 1798–1872. Daughter of the minister of Panbride, the Rev. Dr David Trail, she became a Roman Catholic during a visit to Italy. Ann and her younger friend Margaret Clapperton became novices of the Ursuline order in La Vendee, taking the names Agnes Xavier and Margaret Teresa. The last convent in Edinburgh and the only female community before the Reformation had been that of the Dominicans in The Sciennes†, and now the hierarchy decided to establish a convent of French Ursulines headed by these two Scottish ladies, 'for the education of their own sex, both in the higher classes of society and among the poor, and the relief of the destitute and the sick.' Thus began in 1834 St Margaret's Convent and School in Greenhill. The property and gardens were gifted by Menzies of Pitfodels (*see* Blairs College) who bought Greenhill Cottage nearby for his own residence. Fees at first were 30 guineas a session; uniform consisted of buff gingham in summer and brown stuff in winter with white dresses for Sundays. (*See* P. F. Anson, *Underground Catholicism in Scotland*.) It was not, however, the first Catholic girls' school in the capital as a private seminary called St Mary's had been opened at 14 Scotland Street, by Miss Fraser, former pupil of the Bar Convent at York.

TRAPRAIN LAW. *See* Thenew.

TRIDUANA. *See* Restalrig.

TRINITY CONGREGATIONAL CHURCH, GLASGOW. *See* Hunter, John.

TRISTRAM [Trustram, Trusty]. *See* Drostan.

TULLIBODY. *See* Dick, Robert; Serf.

TWEEDMOUTH. *See* Lee, Robert.

TYNINGHAME. *See* Thenew.

URR (Stewartry of Kirkcudbright). *See* Hepburn, John.

URY (Kincardineshire). *See* Barclay, Robert.

VANORA. *See* Meigle.

WALKER, Mary and **Barbara.** *See* St Mary's Episcopal Cathedral, Edinburgh

WALLACE GREEN CHURCH, BERWICK. *See* Cairns, John.

WARD CHAPEL, DUNDEE. *See* Erskine, Thomas.

WARD, Valentine. 1781–1834. Born at Madeley, Salop, he became a Methodist preacher and served in Scotland, with the exception of three years south of the border, from 1811–28. For most of this time he was Chairman either of the Edinburgh or Aberdeen Districts, and he also served in Glasgow where he led in the erection of three new chapels. The most powerful and popular of the 'second generation' Methodists in Scotland he has been regarded as a mixed blessing to his cause as he had an almost irresistible and irresponsible compulsion to erect huge new chapels, leaving the Church with a burden of debt which took over a generation to pay off. Some of these were very necessary — in Edinburgh the original 'octagon' in the Old Calton was decayed and in 1816 Ward replaced it with the seemly and adequate Nicolson Square building which is still in use. Even there he left debt hanging over the congregation so that as late as 1835 the Town Council gave £3,000 to help to write it off. In Elgin the 30 Methodists found themselves in possession of a chapel seating 1,300: another was erected in the tiny village of Strathkinness. In all, Ward erected or purchased fourteen chapels, many of which were sold or vacated within a generation. When he left Scotland the Methodist Conference sent him round England and Ireland collecting to pay off the debts he had left. He was, however, a popular leader, and before his death had the distinction of having been Chairman of five Districts. In 1834 he left England for missionary work in Jamaica, but the climate killed him within six months.

WARDLAW, James. *See* Erskine, Ralph.

WARR, Alfred. *See* Rosneath.

WATSON, John. *See* Mylne, Andrew.

WELSH, Jane. *See* Irving, Edward.

WESLEY, John. 1703–91. The English evangelist paid no less than 22 visits to Scotland between 1751 and 1790. Every Spring, as regularly as the trees blossomed,

Wesley appeared, sometimes sailing up the east coast to Arbroath (hence, perhaps, the Methodist cause in that town today), sometimes crossing the Solway sands to Annan, at others arriving at Portpatrick from Ulster, and often travelling by one of the highways. The results of so much labour were, however, disappointing and his success in no way comparable with that in other parts of Britain. By 1774 there were only 735 Scottish Methodists and by 1782 the number had shrunk to 459. According to W. F. Swift (*Wesley Hist. Soc. Lectures*), in 1780 Wesley was in despair 'when he remembered his long and troublesome journeys through the land, the abundant labours of his preachers and the money he had so freely poured out his heart was sad and he knew not what to do.' Why had Methodism to struggle for its existence in Scotland at a time when Congregationalism was making rapid progress? Swift suggests: (*i*) its Arminian theology condemned it in the eyes of a Calvinist Scotland; (*ii*) it was administered centrally from south of the border; (*iii*) Scots did not respect itinerant and lay preachers; (*iv*) the people had no choice of a minister. Wesley himself was in something of a dilemma; he felt nearer to the Episcopalians than to the Established Church but realized that to hope for any success his preachers must be acceptable to the Presbyterian majority. He postponed ordaining ministers to preach in Scotland until 1785 and even then tried to convince himself and others that he was in no way separating his people from the Church of Scotland. His two most influential supporters were Dr John Gillies, minister of College Church, Glasgow and Lady Darcy Maxwell, widow of Sir John Maxwell of Pollok and a member of the Edinburgh West Kirk. For only a brief spell did he have the backing of Lady Glenorchy† who did not like his Arminian theology. After 1885 the cause in Scotland took a turn for the better, largely through the devotion of such preachers as Thomas

The 'Totum Kirkie', Wesley's octagonal church at Arbroath

Cherry of Arbroath, Robert Dall† and Duncan Wright. At John Wesley's death there were over 1,000 members, rising to about 4,000 by 1819 but declining to half that number by the middle of the century. *See also* Ward, Valentine.

WHITE, Hugh. *See* Simpson, Elspeth.

WHITEFIELD, George. 1714–70. 'How surprised would be the world if they were to peep upon Dr Squintum and see only a cow-heel upon his table' remarked the great evangelist of his physical disability and his frugal living. He became very corpulent and rather a figure of fun, but in reality he was abstemious in diet and a meticulously tidy person in his habits. Whitefield was son of a Gloucestershire inn-keeper who at Oxford was influenced by the Methodist movement of the Wesleys. He reacted against their strictness and became a convinced Calvinist — one was saved not through methodical prayer or any human effort but by the grace of Christ, sometimes in spite of oneself. His open-air preaching at Moorfields and Kennington attracted very large crowds and caused a great deal both of religious fervour and disrespectful abuse. Although he was an Anglican clergyman who only spent short periods in Scotland, one of his biographers (Robert Philip) claims that 'he deserves a monument on the Calton Hill as the second Reformer of the metropolis'. He visited Scotland first at the invitation of Ralph Erskine† and the Seceders expected him to confine his campaigns to them. When he refused to limit himself in this way they viewed him at first with distrust — Moncrieff† wanted him to disavow his Episcopal ordination — and then with bitterness. Gib, leader of the Seceders in Edinburgh, wrote a pamphlet so vituperative that later he confessed that he was ashamed of it. The more evangelical ministers of the Established Church, Willison of Dundee in particular, were willing to give Whitefield scope for his preaching. He played a prominent part in the Cambuslang† revival.

WHITHORN (Wigtownshire). Far more important historically than first sight of this modest little royal burgh would suggest. Turn into a pend half way down the main street and you have 1,500 years of history before you. (*a*) A museum (AM) with stone crosses dating from around 450, the very oldest in Britain. They should be compared with those at Kirkmadrine† (AM). Together they confirm that there was a Christian centre hereabouts from about the time the Romans left up to the Anglian period in the eighth century. But it has to be noted that there is no inscription to link the stones or the place with Ninian. (*b*) Deep beneath you lies what remains of the Celtic muinntir or settlement of Candida Casa which Professor Ralegh Radford excavated — 'it was the white covering (of the walls) which distinguished the original church of St Ninian and the discovery near the centre of the monastery of a primitive building treated in this manner justifies the deduction that it is indeed the White House, the little church in which the shrine of St Ninian lay for so many centuries.' Other scholars are more sceptical; it could well be the place of the saint's shrine but much later than the original white hut. All we can assert is that from early Christian times there was here, or nearby, a muinntir of the Celtic type, with beehive huts, little oratories, farm buildings and a graveyard, after the model of Skellig Michael in Co. Kerry. (*c*) There was a third phase of which no visible trace remains, the bishopric of Whithorn known to Bede. The Anglian Northumbria annexed Galloway and re-established the old ecclesiastical centre but under their control. The first bishop, Bede says, was Pechthelm. (*d*) Eclipse came to this community with the Norse invasions — the terror of the Black Gentiles (Danes) and the Fair Gentiles (Vikings) — but they in turn accepted Christianity and Whithorn emerged into the mediaeval age with the founding of the Premonstratensian Priory in 1177 (AM). It has one glorious carved doorway. It was an offshoot from Soulseat† and in its turn begat at least two other houses of this order. A bishopric of Galloway was established but Whithorn itself was poorly endowed with few monks. It became an important place of pilgrimage to Ninian's shrine. We learn that pilgrims returning to England were issued with little badges to prove that they had actually made the pilgrimage — antedating the

Romanesque doorway, Whithorn Priory

modern car stickers 'We have visited the Wildlife Park'! The last genuine resident Prior died in 1514, half a century before the Scottish Reformation and here, as elsewhere, 'commendators' filched the revenues for secular purposes. (*e*) Finally, the parish church is worth a visit. Built in 1822 it is not unpleasant if hardly worthy of such glorious antecedents. Before it was built the priory nave was used for parish worship. *See also* Struthers, J. P.

WHITHORN, Isle of (Wigtownshire). Now a peninsula but very near to becoming an island again, as the public was reminded a few years ago when a massive rescue operation had to be launched to prevent the little community being swamped by the Solway tides. On its tip, beyond the whitewashed houses and the harbour, are the faint traces of a rath or earth circle enclosing a mediaeval chapel (AM). Some scholars regarded this as the site of the original Candida Casa, thinking Whithorn itself must have been a slightly later and more developed community. Certainly the Isle would seem to be the likely place for a settlement when sea was the best means of travel and of escape. However, excavations carried out by Professor Charles Thomas have failed to discover any traces of occupation in the

early period of the Church. Once again the archaeologist has shattered the vision of Ninian, Patrick and other saints approaching the little harbour in their curroughs, a vision easily conjured up when one looks out through the lancet window of the chapel towards Ireland and Man. When Whithorn became a place of pilgrimage in mediaeval times the chapel here would be their place for thankful prayer on landing before they took the road for the last few miles to the shrine of the saint. Westward from the Isle, at Physgill, is Ninian's cave. For long neglected, but now well-signposted and cared for by the Ministry of the Environment (AM), it is one of the most romantic and beautiful spots for the Celtic Church student to find and linger in. Various crosses and fragments have been removed for safety to Whithorn museum but there are still traces of early crosses on the walls, enough to make sure that it was the retreat or desertum, if not of Ninian, then of some other early Christian.

WIGTOWN. Our note on Kirkmahoe† suggested that the real patron saint of this burgh is not St Machutus, but ecclesiastical fame has come to Wigtown not because of its patron but because of the alleged drowning of two women in 1685 for their covenanting adherence — Margaret Wilson, aged 16 of Penninghame parish, and Margaret Lauchlison, aged 63, of Kirkinner. A large monument commemorates their martyrdom, tied to stakes at the mouth of the River Bladnoch. In the middle of the last century Sheriff Mark Napier asserted that the execution was never carried out and that the obelisk 'like a tall bully lifts its head and lies.' His book, *Case for the Crown*, was attacked by the parish minister of Glasserton, Archibald Stewart, in *History Vindicated in the Case of the Wigtown Martyrs*. Napier brought to the controversy all the trained expertise of a sheriff in sifting evidence and built up a strong case, especially when a document was discovered in the Register House purporting to grant a temporary reprieve to both women, along with another in which Mistress Lauchlison, recanting her previous views, promised to conform; this last was not signed by her as she was 'scribere necien'. In support of the constant tradition of the drowning, Mr Stewart brought forward not only the sworn testimony of the Presbytery and two kirk-sesssions but also a very weighty tombstone, the date of which, however, was in some doubt.

This now forgotten controversy would provide excellent training for those who desire to argue for or against the historicity of the Gospels, to which problem it presents a close resemblance. There is no doubt that the sentence of drowning was passed and that the women's offence was refusal to abjure the Sanquhar Declaration. If they did not die on Wigtown Sands what happened to them? They disappear from history and obviously they could not have continued to live in the district without it being noted.

WILLIAMSON, Henry. *See* Palmer, Thos. F.

WILLISON, John. 1680–1750. Born near Stirling, Willison's first charge was at Brechin where he faced strong opposition from Jacobite Episcopalians who were very numerous in the district. In 1705 he notified presbytery that the former Episcopalian curate was reoccupying the parish pulpit on Sabbath afternoons, and on complaining to the magistrates he had been told that if he took any action he would be 'rabbled' out of the parish. Perhaps due to this he was all his life strongly anti-Episcopalian, keeping up a pamphlet battle in defence of established Reformed religion. Later, when he was in Dundee, Prince Charles' highlanders threatened to shoot him in the pulpit if he prayed for King George, so he shut his church until the rebellion was over. Transferred in 1716 to the South Kirk, Dundee, he became leader of the 'popular' party in the Assembly, always casting his vote in favour of moderation and tolerance. He was on terms of friendship with the Erskines† and in the Assembly of 1734 moved their reception back into the Church of Scotland. Bitterly disappointed at his failure to heal this schism he withdrew from church politics and restricted himself to writing and to the care of his Dundee parish. He warmly supported the Cambuslang† and Kilsyth revivals. The Dundee church named after him disappeared several years ago but the city still has its Willison Street.

WILSON, Margaret. *See* Wigtown.

WILSON, William. *See* Erskine, Ebenezer.

WILSON, Woodrow. *See* Maxwell, Willielma.

WINZET, Ninian. *c.* 1518–92. The 'z' is, of course, the old Scots 'y' and is so pronounced. 'An Catholike Priest borne in Renfrew' is how he describes himself on the cover of one of his early pamphlets *The Last Blast of the Trumpet*, an obvious rejoinder to Knox's famous blast against the monstrous 'regemen' of women. Much later, when Winzet was writing apologia for the 'old faith' in Latin he signed his *Skirmish Against George Buchanan* as by 'eodem Niniano VVinzeto Renfroo, S. Theologiae doctore.' He seems to have been proud of his Renfrew origin. His early education may have been scanty for he took no degree at Glasgow and writes 'As a theologe I profes me to be nane, nor yit of the nummer of the hie leirnit.' About 1551 he was teaching in Linlithgow and apparently held a chaplaincy in St Michael's Church, a building which suffered badly as it was directly in the path of the Reformers when they marched between Edinburgh and Stirling. It was here that Winzet began disputing with the Protestants in favour of the Catholic views on the Blessed Sarcament, prayers for the dead etc. He refused to subscribe the Scots Confession in 1561 and writes with justifiable indignation that he was therefore 'expellit and schott out of that kyndly town'. His expulsion from Linlithgow coincided with Mary Stuart's return to Scotland and for a time he was attached to her court at Holyrood, perhaps sharing with Benoist the duties of confessor. Forced to leave the country, Winzet stayed for a time in the Low Countries where he continued his controversies, now written in Scots. He disliked Knox's use of English and taxed him with having 'foryet our auld plane Scottis quhilk your mother leirit you'. His last work in Scots, a translation of St Vincent's *Commonitorium* he dedicated to Mary, Queen of Scots. Except for a time when he was called to England to serve Mary in her imprisonment, most of the remainder of his life was spent on the continent. At last he was able to repair his lack of scholarship by study at Paris and Douai, and his last writings were in Latin. It seems that he was able to pay one visit to his beloved Linlithgow, but although banished to foreign parts he found work which could serve both his Church and his native land. In Germany there were several abbeys of Scots foundation which were at a very low ebb. Taking the Benedictine habit, Winzet was appointed abbot of Ratisbon and spent the last fifteen years of his life not only in restoring it physically and spiritually but in recovering the other Scottish abbeys in Germany and Austria. As controversalist, Winzet had not the rapier thrust of Kennedy† but he was frank and fair in admitting that the Scots Church which he so loved had brought her troubles on herself by her own faults and weaknesses.

WOOD, Alexander [Lang Sandy]. *See* Hay, George.

WOODROW, Thomas. *See* Maxwell, Willielma.

WORDSWORTH, Charles. 1806–92. Nephew of the poet, son of the scholar Christopher, brother of the Christopher who became Bishop of Lincoln, and uncle of John, Bishop of Salisbury. He was probably the only person in the history of the modern church who managed to vote himself into the Apostolic Succession. His first appointment in Scotland (1847) was as the first warden of Glenalmond — founded with Gladstone's help to save the sons of Episcopal gentry from being educated by Presbyterians. Wordsworth, who had been a pupil at Harrow and was teaching at Winchester, organized the new foundation on English public school lines. Marion Lochhead (*Episcopal Scotland*) writes 'He came north enveloped in the mantle of William of Wykeham which he tried to drape round the shoulders of young Scots.' As Warden he had a vote in selecting a Bishop for the see of St Andrews, Dunblane and Dunkeld, in the Episcopal Church, and when the vote fell to be exercised in 1853 Wordsworth cast it for himself. Not unnaturally this caused not merely resentment but active opposition on the part of many clergy, especially the chapter of his own cathedral at Perth. The feeling was not assuaged when for a year he refused to relinquish the Glenalmond appointment. The controversy between bishop and clergy clouded many of the years of his life and at one point led to his removing his chair from St Ninian's Cathedral to St John's Church in Perth. Undoubtedly he had a generous measure of what would today be termed 'personality and communication difficulties' but he should also be remembered as one of the few Episcopal clergy of his day — and the only Bishop — who tried to understand and express his respect for ministers of the National Church, among whom Principal Tulloch and Dr Norman Macleod† were his friends. He passed a more happy retirement at St Andrews where he is buried.

WOTHERSPOON, H. J. *See* Lee, Robert.

WRANGHOLM (Smailholm). *See* Cuthbert.

WRIGHT, Duncan. *See* Dall, Robert.

WYNTOUN. *See* Serf.

XAVIER, Sister Agnes. *See* Trail, Ann Agnes.

YOUNG, Gavin. *See* Ruthwell Cross.

ZINZERNDORFF, Nikolaus von. *See* Caldwell, John.